Multiple Streams of Income

How to Diversify Your Career and Protect Yourself, Your Income, and Your Future Even in Hard Economic Times

Chris Lutz

Copyright © 2015 Lutz

All rights reserved.

ISBN: 1514868989
ISBN-13: 978-1514868980

DEDICATION

To all my entrepreneur friends and supporters, my parents for their support and giving me a great start in life. And especially to you, the hard-working reader, whom I hope to help inspire to make the world, especially America, a better place. And, of course, to Harvey Mackay.

CONTENTS

	Acknowledgments	7
1	An Entrepreneur's Perspective	8
2	The Awakening	16
3	Business Cycle Management	18
4	Solutions	30
5	My Multiple Streams	37
6	You Can Do This Too	41
7	Get Started Today	46
8	The Rewards	49
9	Successful Consulting	52
10	How to Get into Freelancing and Consulting	57
11	Where to Look for Multiple Customers	64
12	Working at Home? Time is of the Essence!	67
13	Save Money, Deal With Cash Crises, and Spend Less Than Your Competitors	74
14	Automated Revenue Streams	78
15	Additional Resources	94
16	Appendix	102

Multiple Streams of Income

ACKNOWLEDGMENTS

A special thanks to Harvey Mackay and others for inspiring me down this life path.

1 AN ENTREPRENEUR'S PERSPECTIVE

"You must understand that it is not only possible, but highly desirable, to do several things simultaneously; thus, it happened that I was operating an international airline, importing thousands of live wild animals, producing films for television and building exercise machines all at the same time. In my opinion, many of our current problems are direct results of specialization ..."

Arthur Jones – Entrepreneur, film maker, inventor of Nautilus exercise equipment

In high school I read a business book by Harvey Mackay. From then on I knew I wanted to be an entrepreneur. I've since had the good fortune of co-authoring this business book so that others can learn from my experience. This is the fulfillment of a dream. Read on and open your mind to the possibilities of a different kind of work life.

Many Americans have been making a huge mistake for decades. We've bought into things that others have told us about without verifying facts or thinking critically. We have had unrealistic expectations. We have some degree of narcissism. And we have become entitled. Rarely do we see alternative ways of doing things when, in fact, there are probably an infinite number of paths to our desired destinations.

Worst of all, as a culmination of all those factors, we've become part of the "working dead." Those are the people who trudge to work every day in a zombie-like state and continue on that path for years. Some never awaken from this state.

That's the awesome power of a culture; the ability to perpetuate itself without active interference, whether it be a business culture or the American culture as a whole. Just think, how can a company afford to pay a pension to employees who have worked for 30 or 40 years, or more? Pretty soon, the company will be paying more people who are NOT working for them than people who ARE. Do you see the flaw in this system?

Today, with people living longer, it doesn't take much to eat up a lot of money quickly. Following the disastrous effects of the global financial crises and several years of recession-like conditions, many may need to live without the pension that was expected to fund them for the last decades of their lives. This applies to both public and private sectors. Trusting relationships are difficult to find.

Yes, it's good to specialize in a profession, but consider this for a moment: few people would ever invest even a single dollar without "diversifying" it. *Why, then, do we do exactly the opposite with our regular income which may be more important to our short term stability?* If you're spending your whole life working for someone else for a fraction of the revenue and a vision that is not your own, you're paddling against the current. You're helping to enrich others. That's not a terrible thing, but consider a job where you could take more ownership of the end product and reap more of the benefit. Or make that your own company or side venture part time. That's really what we're going to delve into in this book. How you can avoid putting all of your eggs in one basket and avoid any major pitfalls along the path of your career that may be out of your control.

My Backstory

I wanted to be an entrepreneur since I was about 12 years old. It's not always this clear so early for others. I tried to follow the conventional wisdom and advice of that era: go to school, graduate, get a good job, and save for retirement. That might be good for some and things may have worked well under that formula for decades. But it's dead now!

Here's another problem: I get bored easily. I could not imagine having the same job for 10, 20, 30, or 40 years. Usually, over two to five years, I feel like I've got a really good handle on something and look for more challenges.

I have also never felt entirely comfortable working for others. It wasn't that I was a bad employee. I may have been better than others because I understood both sides of the situation. But I'm not a great manager as I often expect co-workers to be like me. I have trouble recognizing and isolating the motivations of others.

Decisive and fast are my catch-words. I'm eternally optimistic; things don't bother me even when they should. Big pictures are easy but I have trouble with details. I'm working on that. These are classic entrepreneurial traits that I've found and seen in others to whom I relate.

When I was younger and played sports, I was fairly good at ice hockey and went as far as I could. Every kid likes to think they would make it to the professional league of their sport. Of course, I wanted to make it to the NHL, however unlikely it was. In my early teens I specifically remember my Dad saying to me: "Why play when you can own the team?"

He explained that although the players got all the on-ice glory, it was the owners of the professional teams who really did well. And if I thought pro players made a lot of money, the owners made exponentially more. I didn't fully understand that at first, but what he said resonated with me. If nothing else, it was certainly an easier approach; easier on the body rather than a full-time job in a full contact sport where injuries and fist fights are a daily occurrence.

I wasn't an exceptional student. I was slightly above average which I believe is characteristic of a lot of entrepreneurs. There were flashes of brilliance when the right things came together. I thought I didn't like reading in school. Now, I can read a book a week. It just so happened that what I was forced to read didn't match my interests or passions.

In fictional stories I find it difficult to visualize plot movements and often get lost. However, in high school, I was drawn to a sports marketing class. Having previously considered a career in Public Relations, or ideally, representing players as a sports agent, I was interested in the course. I even interviewed the parent of a teammate who was an agent for a professional player. That class held my attention. It was a prerequisite for an advanced marketing class I took as a senior in high school. I did very well in this class which offered me the opportunity to read something I would enjoy immensely, and more importantly, learn a lot from. It was Harvey Mackay's *Swim with the Sharks Without Being Eaten Alive: Outsell, Outmanage, Outmotivate, and Outnegotiate Your Competition*. I loved that book and still do.

That was in 1996 and I still get his weekly emails. From that single book I learned a lot about management techniques, negotiation (everything is negotiable), and how to make an unexciting business – like envelopes and paper – stand out. Mostly, though, I learned more about myself. Entrepreneurship was my likely destiny.

I held several jobs while in high school, through college, and after I graduated which allowed me to gain valuable experience and move into leadership roles. Although not a control freak, I typically like to work alone and have a lot of ideas and energy. I hate to be confined.

As someone else's employee I am not able to manage the power in the relationship. In fact, I disagree – massively – with the traditional American way firms are organized and run. In many organizations much of the labor is so far removed from the customer that employees don't care. They can't see the overall vision, process or outcome. They lose the feeling of ownership in what they are doing. Soon, they join the ranks of the "working dead."

Labor then becomes resentful of management and ownership. Ownership resents labor. Quality of service plummets and customers stop patronizing the business. Many of us live in free countries with individual rights and freedoms to do what we want. But businesses are set up like monarchies or some kind of caste system. Naturally, a worker prefers not to have an overbearing master or to be bossed around. Yet, in a business, that is often exactly what occurs.

With someone else in charge of my efforts, direction, and, most importantly, my pay, I was uncomfortable and unhappy in the past. In fact, in my last "employed" job early in the new millennium, my pay changed drastically three times in three years. My income was wildly out of my control. I understand the need for it to change due to business conditions but I couldn't plan ahead and had no financial regularity whatsoever.

I'm fine without regular income, as long as I can do something to change my circumstances. I've never had a salary because I was always working on commission. I didn't want a salary. My concern was always the potential upside or how much commission I could make as a direct result of my efforts. In the second year of my "employed" job, I had to work about 25 per cent more to make just under what I had the previous year. Client appointments were at the client's mercy so it wasn't like I worked 10 or 12 hours straight all the time, although it was possible. Sometimes appointments were spread from 5 am or 6 am all the way through 8 pm or 8.30 pm.

Typically, I saw clients in the early morning, for a few hours in the middle of the day, and from afternoon into the late evening. That's how it was. Obviously, this burned me out.

With some control over my schedule I tried to optimize it as best I could. Despite holding a management position I was also handling most of the client appointments – often up to 90 a week. As I had no problem securing new client referrals I suggested to my boss that I work straight through from 6 am to 3 pm each day – a nine-hour day plus half a day on Saturday.

He said: "Well, you need to be here for the busy evenings." It was clear that the only goal was to get more clients. No matter how many clients we had, it seemed it was never enough.

A typical day for me would sometimes stretch to 14 hours. So the following year it was either continue to burn out or work more reasonable hours. The latter meant nearly a $20,000 pay cut, excluding management pay. On this commission-only job I was paid $30 an hour which although a reasonable rate necessitated about 90 client sessions a week just to cover expenses. Keep in mind, this was Loudoun County, Virginia, then the highest median income county in the nation at $115,500 a year per household. I knew of competitors working for themselves nearby who charged $60 to $100 an hour for the same service in less well-off areas.

In early to mid-2000 I also had other business interests so I started cultivating some of them. One was a fishing lure side business I wanted to start with my father. It centered around an ecommerce website. One day a co-worker warned that my boss thought I was spending time on that at the expense of my job.

My co-worker, in the same financial situation as me, explained on my behalf: "Well, he has to supplement his income." Why? Because our pay rates changed three times in three years. That was a turning point. I had no power over my own pay even though I was working more than ever. Worse, it was apparently not unreasonable to dedicate outlandish hours to pursuing clients. I realized I couldn't centralize that earning power with someone else or an organization that wasn't mine.

This type of job was not for me. It would cost me the time I wanted to devote to many other interests. My life had become a dull routine, working long hours, going home, stuffing my face with food, going immediately to bed and then returning to work in the early morning. I needed to be in control of my time, or at least have some recourse if things didn't go the way I liked. I was in business to make something work on its own, not keep piling more on my own plate.

At the start of this chapter I quoted Arthur Jones who is well known for his contribution to the fitness industry, the Nautilus line of equipment machines. Arthur was an eccentric, Howard Hughes-type personality. He had many passions that included making films for National Geographic, capturing wildlife, and aviation. I've heard stories that he ran his Nautilus company as a very free and fluid work environment where employees gravitated to the departments in which they were interested. Somehow, they still produced. Jones also combined his passions by keeping aircraft and wild animals, such as elephants and crocodiles, on the Nautilus property, sometimes to the dismay of customers and visitors.

He considered specialization somewhat evil as it caused people, like the physicians in his family, to view the world only through what they were taught and little else. For example, he felt that those in the medical field did not view or understand proper exercise principles. He preferred a generalist approach to life, a concept that can also apply to work life.

Self-Reflection Questions and Actions

1. **What are the benefits and drawbacks of working as an employee? What feels right? What feels awkward or difficult?**

2. **What are the benefits and drawbacks of working for yourself? What feels right? What feels awkward or difficult?**

3. **Actions: Allow your intuitive responses to the previous questions to drive your decision process. If you intuitively wish to be self-employed, list two actions you can take now to move in that direction. Or, if you intuitively wish to be an employee, list two specific actions you can take now to move in that direction.**

Please note that if you want to be an entrepreneur but cannot bear the perceived risks, another option is to work entrepreneurially within an organization or as a contractor, building and launching new projects, products, and programs.

2 THE AWAKENING

While one specialization is useful, I've come to realize it is better to have several. Any investor would feel at risk putting 100 per cent of his money into one area. But that's exactly what we are doing by working full time for one employer and leaving all the power in the relationship with them. Most people would say that they can't rely their employer to look after their interests. It's the nature of some businesses that things may need to change quickly and those things might include your job or your pay.

Nor can you rely on things to stay the same in the long term. Most people dislike change. However, we need to make a little room in our lives for accepting it, or better yet, being excited about it. Many times when people are forced into a change they otherwise would not have made, they eventually like it. This often happens with jobs. An employee may never have left a company but after being laid off found a better position elsewhere with more pay. Change can be good and exciting. Don't be afraid of it.

Who's to say your employer couldn't take all your ideas and creativity for its own use then "let you go" the next day? It happens. Worse, if you have a non-compete clause in your exit conditions you can't start the same business in the same area. You're essentially someone else's property in that situation. Your intellectual property might be considered theirs too, depending on the relationship you had.

While it's a shame, nearly every employer will look at the balance sheet and see payroll on the liability side. But those people (payroll) are also producing revenue in a lot of businesses. Of course that doesn't matter when things are tight and costs need to be cut. If a business is set up properly with all the right people, the payroll is the biggest asset rather than the biggest liability.

But, that's not how things appear to work with a lot of employers. If your position or job is on the liability side of the balance sheet, you'll be looked at as a risk rather than an asset to your company.

Self-Reflection Questions and Actions

1. How can multiple specializations help you better serve your clients or employer?

2. What special skills do you have that could provide value to prospective clients or employers? List as many as possible.

3. Create an online profile at www.LinkedIn.com including all your special skills. These are key words, which a prospective employer or client will use to conduct a search to find you. If you already have an online profile, update it to specifically reflect these key words.

4. At www.LinkedIn.com, conduct a test, searching on the key words within your own profile. Review the types of resumes and job opportunities that your search yields. Continue to refine your own online profile so that others can find you. Update your profile again with any new key words that you discovered from your search.

3 BUSINESS CYCLE MANAGEMENT

In America today, capitalism often gets a bad reputation and poor press. Even though, that is essentially what allowed us to become the most prosperous nation on the planet in record time. But, that's beside the point. That was then, this is now. It isn't quite accurate to say America is capitalistic any more. Robert Kiyosaki referred to our current system as a form of "creditism." I'd say that's probably true.

But, regardless of what you call it, it is true nowadays that it isn't just about going out there and working hard, or getting a good education, or you'll succeed if you have a good plan. The latter may be true, but probably not in the sense that I'm talking about. What I'm referring to is business cycle management.

There have been many people who have been utterly destroyed by being caught in a place in the economy at a bad time.

Business cycles can have different definitions, but in a nutshell, it is an expansion and contraction of the economy in succession. They aren't always predictable and they aren't always over similar time periods. And they don't always occur across the economy as a whole. Different segments of the economy and even different individuals and localities can be affected at different times.

Basically, banks control the money. The federal government prints the money and largely controls the banks. But, the banks, also control the government to some extent. The government, in a central planning effort, attempts to control the flow of money to certain areas of the economy or the country at different times.

Rather than this being based naturally on demand and real

economic activity, it is a sort of artificial redirection of money and resources to a certain area based on someone's idea or whims legally.

What happens when the federal government showers an area with money? Businesses crop up, everyone buys a house, and lives the good life...seemingly. As long as that flow of money is open, things will likely be good. But, if that flow gets shut off or diverted, and there wasn't a real economic reason for continued economic activity in that area to begin with and absorb the diversion, then you'll see a crash. People lose their jobs, housing values go down, business go bankrupt.

The boom and bust cycle. We've all seen it. Some generations more than others. The booms tend to be bigger and the busts more heart breaking as time goes on the more the government manipulates the money supply and the flow of money. Most recently we all remember the housing bubble; a combination of poor credit lending practices by the financial institutions and poor governance by the government that either forced them to or allowed them to do it. Soon after that we had a major financial crisis. The stock market DJIA was close to 7000. One of the lowest points since the Great depression. At time of writing this, it is over 18000. Do you think every penny of that is real? Of course not. The funneling of money to certain areas of the economy is sowing the seeds for the next bust.

In this day and age, the trick for you, as a savvy entrepreneur or businessperson, is to be able to effectively see, navigate, and manage these business cycles.

There are certain data points that can help you determine what areas and customers are good candidates for you and what areas and customers might only be propped up temporarily by an infusion of money.

When the federal reserve increases the money supply (inflation), it doesn't go out into the economy evenly. It creates hot spots where there are times of more prosperity.

You want to look for the evidence of where this money is flowing. I'm not talking about just chasing trends here. It's more about avoiding areas and customers that will experience recessions or major contractions in their economies. Think of it like an economic game of hot lava. Only try to step where you are reasonably certain there is a good foundation for footing underneath. Should you step where the flow of money has dried up, you may find that your customer base dries up very quickly too if you are dependent on them locally.

Worse still, is that the people who come into this money first are the most well off. Those that come into it later are hurt the most. When money is directed to an area, the people receiving spend it, prices will subsequently rise. These people get to spend it before prices rise. The people who come into it later have to spend it after prices rise. Their incomes don't rise as fast as prices do. This isn't a good customer, business location/opportunity, or investment for you.

People may eventually become wise to the situation and spend rapidly. They know the money loses value the more they hold it. It's a high velocity of money environment and could lead to a hyperinflation. The government may recognize this and shut down the flow of money to those areas. The people that committed to living and working in these areas later may be left out in the cold.

An important note here. I'm not talking about paying attention to forecasts or opinions on where the economy will be going. That is unreliable and only opinions. We want to look at data. Either published data from other organizations or simple numbers and information you can gather yourself. Published data from other organizations is not always reliable either. The federal government routinely changes its formula for calculating certain economic measures, possibly to suit a particular economic agenda at the time. So you can take that for what it is worth. But, this can be a good place to start on a macro scale and drill down further into more reliable sources of info

The worst of all scenarios is being in an area where the government takes out more in taxes than it puts back in. This is a no win situation for anybody. You don't want to be in a location like this and you don't want to sell to these people who are.

All of this happens naturally in a totally free economy, but to much less extent. It is the small differential in areas that drives an equalizing force of transactions. Resources are diverted from one area to another due to supply and demand and the individual value of each item a given individual assigns it in their own mind. The flow of money in that scenario is often referred to as the "invisible hand."

The most stable and permanent area in the country where you can 100% depend on a steady flow of money is Washington D.C. Or just outside it in the surrounding suburbs. That's where I come from. As long as the federal government is in business, there will forever be a steady waterfall of money across this area.

Even during the most recent housing bubble and financial crisis, my business did well. That's because I lived in that area where many of our clients had government jobs or worked for government contractors. Or they benefitted from the money those organizations received. All of them were much less likely to lose their jobs and need to quit being our customer. Granted, the feeling at the time was one of crisis, but in a real sense, we continued with business pretty much as usual. Between living in that area (geographic hot spot), having that demographic as a clientele (demographic hot spot), and having them all on automatic recurring credit card payments (credit) allowed us to navigate those crises reasonably well. We weren't nearly as phased as many other parts of the country were.

Many times these hot spots are created deliberately through law. But, there are often even more accidental effects too. You can profit from these, but they are much more unpredictable.

Other times, hot spots can develop before the government directs money there. Sometimes this happens due to inaccurate forecasts or hype. People believe it, flock there, set up shop, and nothing ever happens. It's completely hollow and no money ever comes. Be skeptical of this type of forecast or report in a given area or for a certain demographic.

This is most important when it comes to your sales. You're looking for real demand. Always qualify your potential customers.

How to navigate the hot spots.

Classify your sources of income:

Deliberate (by law)

Accidental:

    Accidental full (overflow or over production)

    Accidental hollow (forecasts, hype)

Formula for sales:

1. Find out exactly who the customers are.
2. Find out exactly what they want.
3. Find a way to acquire or produce it.
4. Tell them you can supply them.
5. Remind them of the benefits.
6. Ask for the sale.

The more accuracy in the research you find about your customers the better. You may not need to be to the letter accurate depending on what you do or sell. Geographic or demographic data on a broad scale may be good enough.

If you work as an employee, be SURE that you know everything there is to know about your employer who you are selling your labor to. Know their sources of income, if it is deliberate or accidental, and the relative, near term stability of your job. Will they be able to afford keeping your on?

A customer in a deliberate hot spot is a good customer. They will have more reliable income than someone or a business in accidental hot spots.

An accidental hot spot may have more money at first, but you can't count on it for the long term. Stick and move on these customers.

Let's rank order in terms of reliable incomes.

DF1 (Deliberate Federally created)	SS retirees, military pensioners, civil service pensioners
DS1 (Deliberate State created)	State pensioners.

*Difference: The feds can print money. States cannot. These are not quite as reliable.	
DL1 (Deliberate Locally created)	City and county pensioners.
DF2 (Deliberate Federally created) * Federal money, but subject to budget cuts, layoffs, career changes.	Federal agencies and employees.
DS2 (Deliberate State created)	State agencies or employees.
DL2 (Deliberate Locally created)	Local agencies or employees.
DF3 (Deliberate Federally created) *Incomes don't fluctuate with business cycle, but don't grow with it either. Subject to cuts and layoffs.	Firm or person who sells directly to the federal government or DF1 or DF2. Military contractors, retailers outside military bases, group insurance selling to federal employees.
DS3 (Deliberate State created) *Incomes don't fluctuate with business cycle, but subject to cuts and layoffs.	Firm or individual who sells directly to DS1's and DS2's.
DL3 (Deliberate Locally	Firm or individual who sells

created)	directly to DL1's and DL2's.
AF (Accidental full)	Farmers with over abundance of subsidies, investors flocking to a certain commodity, stock market bubbles.
AH (Accidental hollow)	People and businesses flocking to an area or building because an impending boom that never materializes.
S (Sinkhole) *Areas with high tax burden and little or nothing received. A net loss for them.	Slums or poverty stricken areas. You don't want to sell here, but may buy from these areas.

Some people and businesses are more sensitive to the business cycle than others. Sellers of smaller ticket items are usually not as affected. Businesses that have to go into debt or heavy capital to produce their goods can be particularly sensitive to the business cycle. You can classify your potential customers further on the basis of sensitivity.

Real estate can often be an early warning indicator. It's the largest purchase people make and has the biggest changes when the money supply changes either up or down in a geographical area.

To summarize your plan:

Identify the sources of your income.

    1. Classify them.

2. Determine how vulnerable it makes you to the business cycle.

3. Try to adjust your clientele to a more stable proportion.

4. During downturns, concentrate on your deliberate federally created hot spots or customers. During booms reach out and try to profit in the short term from your accidental hot spots, but don't depend on them.

This is all especially useful if you plan to have a "light" business. What I mean by that is not a capital "heavy" business. A business that is light and agile and can adapt quickly to the conditions at hand. Long term commitments and responsibilities and payments that have to be made can sometimes bleed over into very undesirable downturn conditions and you're stuck. It could cause you to go broke.

Ideally, you don't want a lot of overhead or fixed costs. In a perfect world, you'd only have variable costs or costs that you incur only if you are actually doing business.

You might think the guy with the huge factory, hundreds of workers, and tons of equipment is "rich." He might be…for now. He could also easily not be next month. You never know. But, one thing is for certain, taking all of that on is a much larger risk than many people are willing to take. Somebody has to do it, but not everybody. That isn't what is necessary now. We live in the information age now.

It isn't safe investing a lot of time, money, and capital up front in an uncertain economic environment. We aren't likely to return to that any time soon. So for now, one of the safest routes you can take is an internet business with low start up and low fixed costs.

You can easily act as a middle man, outsource, or dropship products and services of all kinds. You can do a lot with just a computer, a phone, and the mail. This can keep all of your fixed costs as low as possible and what you need to break even low too. Hopefully, you can acquire some DF1 customers who are steady and reliable and can cover those few fixed costs you do have.

Some other good rules of thumb:

1. Don't buy a house or business building. Rent them, preferably for shorter terms. If a deep recession hits, you can adapt and move to a less expensive building. How many people do you know currently still having trouble with real estate they bought prior to 2006 either in business or personally?

2. Don't use debt financing. Only use debt intelligently. For instance, for inventory you know you can immediately sell. You can consider equity financing or personal banking methods. If a recession hits, you can reduce your debt burden if sales diminish.

3. Try to avoid long term projects and commitments if possible. You don't want to get into a huge, multi-year project only to be stuck when the economy turns South. Try to keep your focus to a year or less while still keeping an eye on the future for a longer term vision.

4. Make a real effort to be on the other side of risk. Save and invest during prosperous times. Build a cash cushion or very liquid assets. You can buy up other companies' assets during downturns as they liquidate. Then sell high when the economy recovers. If you know all of your commitments are a year or less, try to know that you have

at least that much to cover you should the worst happen

5. Try to own nothing that ties you down or fixes you to one locality only. In a centrally controlled economy, real estate is the riskiest of all. It could make you rich, but it could make you broke at a moment's notice too.

6. Specialization is good, but don't make it the only thing you're known for or good at. Try to consider yourself, and convey to others that you're a professional entrepreneur. If you have a specialized full time job, be a part time entrepreneur who seeks all opportunities.

If you would like help in your firm's management of the business cycle or learning how to classify customers, you can talk to one of our consultants who are available for training on the subject.

Resources to use for acquiring data:

NTIS Look for the geographic distribution of federal funds. Usually listed by state.

http://lesko.com/ Infousa. Shows you how to contact government experts on every subject imaginable.

www.census.gov. Geographic and demographic data.

http://research.stlouisfed.org/fred2/. Geographic and demographic data.

http://www.directmail.com/mailinglists/. Virtually all the data needed to effectively navigate the business cycle.

http://profitpenguins.com/special/ Use Profit Penguin to easily arbitrate service providers with customers.

Reference: Maybury, Richard. "The Clipper Ship Strategy." Blue Stocking Press, Placerville, CA.

4 SOLUTIONS

Most people want to earn more money. And people, generally, are split into two categories. There are those who bring results after they are promised wealth first and then there are those who bring the results first, and are rewarded afterwards.

Let's explore the two groups in depth. In the first, those who only take action after promises of fat paychecks are more like employees, freshmen, or mercenaries. There is no right or wrong with this kind of thinking, but consider this: you are once again trading your precious time for money. Instead of investing your time in an ASSET that generates money, you spend your time working on something that is short term, for limited wealth, and which does not give you income long after you have stopped working.

Consider also that this kind of short term vision will only produce limited or temporary results, at best. Have you ever seen a security guard asleep at work when the boss is not around? Whenever an employee is offered a higher salary, more medical benefits and longer vacations, the heart starts pumping faster. That is evidence of how emotions rule our chase for the dollar.

A higher salary doesn't mean fewer financial problems though. On the contrary, when your income goes up, your commitments, your tax bracket and the time spent at your workplace increases. The greater your salary, the weaker your position. If your boss is paying you a six figure income and calls an emergency meeting, you had better rush to the office, even if you are half asleep!

A good definition of an employee/boss relationship is this: an employee will only do the bare minimum to keep the boss from firing them and a boss will only pay the bare minimum to keep an employee from leaving. Ok, that's not entirely true, but somewhere there in the middle is the "market price" of this relationship.

The second group includes many creative people – inventors, entrepreneurs, business leaders, creators, innovators, consultants, proprietors, and inventors who, typically, generate a lot of ideas.

To succeed, those in the second group need to stop working for money. What does this mean? Isn't making money part and parcel of having good financial IQ?

What I mean by 'stop working for money' is not working for free. Work, instead, to gain the necessary skills you need to be a successful entrepreneur (or inventor, investor). To illustrate: if you lack the contacts for running a business, the best place to look for contacts is where? Your competitor's customers, of course.

How about product knowledge? Work with a company that can teach you of the skills and the tricks of the trade.

Not familiar with the production line of a factory? Work in one! Learn the ropes, or manage the factory workers.

Fearful of talking to people? Get a sales job where you will be forced to talk all the time. Join a public speaking club like Toastmasters International or Dale Carnegie. This is also a great way to develop perseverance!

The best education you can get is in real life – not in a classroom.

However, remember this: not everybody has what it takes to succeed as an entrepreneur!

Many lack the perseverance, the creative mindset, the financial capabilities or the necessary contacts to get the job done. Some give up too early before any results can be seen! The fastest way to get those skills to succeed is to learn them hands on and get paid in the process! Don't be sidetracked by how much you are paid.

When Donald Trump was selecting candidates in *The Apprentice*, he set their first task: go to the streets and sell lemonade! Many would find it degrading. But to The Donald, it was very important. If you can't do something as simple as sell lemonade, how can you handle a daunting task like running the Trump empire?

Again, let me ask: would you trade time for short term money (money that stops coming in when you stop)?

Or, would you trade time and money for a long term asset that generates income (even long after you have stopped)?

Every problem is an opportunity in disguise. All we need is to look around and find problems to overcome.

It's up to you. You may or may not see the results in the short term, but by using your brain and available resources, you can create true value for which others are willing to pay.

Three Ways of Making Money

It's quite simple.

1. Trade time for money – employees, self-employed.

2. Manifest and use creative ideas – inventors, artists, programmers, and innovators.

3. Leverage resources and other people – business people, leaders.

If you are a professional, have you explored writing an ebook about your field of expertise? If well written, it could provide a new income stream, instead of you selling out your time serving your clients.

How about a computer programmer? You can produce your own revolutionary product or software instead of selling your ideas to the company for which you work.

How about real estate? Instead of selling homes, you could pool financial sources to buy cheap houses, increase their value with inexpensive updates and sell them off at a higher price. It just takes a little time and research to find good ideas.

Is money a problem? Seek loans if you can take the risk. Pool money from investors or seek a grant. The sky is the limit.

Which way do you want to achieve wealth? Answer: it's totally up to you.

A lot of people are opposed to change, even if it's for the better. Many situations persist simply because "it's the way we've always done it" or "this is just how it's done."

Consider whether there might be one or multiple other ways to go about your life rather than what "conventional wisdom" dictates. Might there be a way around the status quo? Yes, of course, there is. There are probably infinite ways to design your life.

I tend to not follow norms and usually buck trends. Just because "everyone else does it that way" could mean I do something different simply out of spite. Call it what you want; trendsetting, not following the herd, or perhaps a slightly rebellious attitude. I don't want to be a member of the "working dead."

An entrepreneurial economy is what made America great. People didn't come to settle the country several hundred years ago for all the good paying jobs. There weren't any. There was nothing but natural resources (they thought there was a lot more gold than there was) and opportunities. Many enterprising individuals recognized the opportunities in tobacco. Even the months it took to ship goods and currency thousands of miles across oceans wasn't off-putting. People were merchants. They had specialized skills and performed the requisite services and were also intimately connected to their customers. They could see the direct relationship between the quality of their efforts and the rewards for those efforts.

Immigrants continue to arrive in America for the freedom to pursue the many opportunities that remain. Sadly, many Americans have become blind to opportunities. Instead, many play the blame game.

"It's the government's fault. It's corporate America's fault. It's (insert your favorite scapegoat's name here) fault." Listen to your friends talk. Perhaps you have been guilty of such thinking.

It's antiquated to think of landing one "secure" job and saving for retirement. We have already established that there is no security. Any feeling of security is an illusion – even if you think you are protected by the law or by being a member of an organization like a union. Anything could happen at any time. The law may say one thing, but there's no guarantee that you'll ever receive a remedy. As long as you are strictly someone's employee at one company, you're a liability on the balance sheet. I say that as a business owner. We cannot trust any government to provide us with what we need, nor is that its responsibility. We cannot trust most employers either. Insulate yourself with multiple incomes either from different companies or by working for yourself in addition to one main source of income. Diversify and protect yourself.

Specialization is good, but diversification is better. Have two or three specializations. This sounds a lot harder than it is. I'm not saying you now need two or three full-time jobs, but we are all likely to have several areas of interest or even passion. You're likely participating in pursuits centered around those interests already. Is there any way that you might be able to profit from those interests and passions? While it might not result in money at first, work out how your interest or passion may benefit you in another way apart from enjoyment or recreation.

It is important that when designing this part of your life, you don't take something you love and turn it into something you hate by making it seem like work. Let's take my custom kayak fishing rod revenue stream as an example. If I had to market, prospect, hunt down leads, try to turn them into paying customers, build the rods myself then ship them off, I'd probably hate it. I do market them, but as it turns out, I meet a lot of people who are interested in the same activity. I use my product. It's visible. Others can see it and feel it. The conversation will turn to how they can get one of my rods. I can give them a business card where they can order straight from my website.

Alternatively, I may sell one on the spot. I do not manufacture them myself. I enjoy the design process but I have a someone who procures the parts and assembles them for me under my label. That's the hard part. All I have to do is order them, mark them up 100 per cent on our website, sell them, and ship them off. Interacting with the customers is fun and easy, an activity we all enjoy. It's not a lot of work for me. If I had to do all parts of the process myself, I probably wouldn't do it for very long. So think about how you can take your passions and interests and turn them into a revenue stream that doesn't require a whole day of your time.

Everyone can cultivate at least one "side stream" or specialization that interests them. This does not need to be a full-on business for which you perform every function. It can take the form of consulting, or using a skill as a sole proprietor after which you pay taxes on your earned income. Experience one side stream and then hopefully add more.

Another key point is that if your primary source of income is employment in another company, be sure of exactly what that entails. You don't want to engage in anything that violates the terms of your employment or competes with your employer. That might provide immediate grounds for your dismissal. On the flip side, there may be no problem in pursuing outside income streams. However, don't let your current employer know. It's none of their business. Unless you are dedicating your life to that company 24/7, you may be disparaged if you engage in other pursuits. Just continue working as usual without letting on.

Self-Reflection Questions

1. **This chapter lists 3 different ways of earning income. Find that list and note which group you gravitate most towards. If you are currently in one group, yet feel yourself outgrowing it and gravitating towards another group, note that too.**

2. **Identify a "side stream" that you can add to the current way you do business.**

3. **Identify at least two actions you can take to move in the direction of developing a "side stream."**

5 MY MULTIPLE STREAMS

I launched a fitness company providing one-on-one personal training. I then branched out to consult and serve the rest of the fitness industry with business-to-business offerings in the form of business management tools, systems, and organizing their operations. I then expanded my focus to offer these tools, systems and services to small business owners.

Secondarily, I own a fishing lure and custom kayak fishing rod and guide service company which is run through a website. There are few significant fixed or up-front costs. Nearly all the costs are variable, meaning that costs arise only if money is made first. I also lead fun, guided trips with clients who pay quite well. This venture was created as a project to share with my father which could also potentially offer him activity and income as he approached retirement age.

I would not have designed the custom kayak fishing rod had I not listened to my internal cues after years spent pursuing my favorite pastime—fishing. I have an intense drive to turn my passions into revenue streams from which I can profit. Allowing those passions to combine with business sense produced a new product for a growing industry.

Another website I own promotes resources for entrepreneurs. Everything available from this site is virtual information products and/or membership. Again, costs are nearly 100 per cent variable. Nor is there an inventory of products to house or manage. Electronically-available products provide customers with a supply that never runs out. Information is always available on the website. I continue to explore new ways to monetize this site.

I have done some affiliate marketing, created a web form to build an email list for marketing, and placed some hard copy and ebooks for sale in the $27 to $39 price range. There is very little upkeep and maintenance necessary. If you set up a revenue stream like this, it's a great feeling when you get emails informing you you're nearly $100 richer from a product sold that you did nothing additional to make happen.

You might go to sleep and someone on the other side of the world purchases something you put together with your knowledge and passion. That's just a few sales. You want to multiply that by a few more. Imagine doing just five of those a day. If you did that over five days a week, you just made yourself an extra $600 dollars a week which is $2,400 a month. I'm not saying it's that easy, but it is possible. It all depends on the traffic you can direct to the website. It would be nice to have an extra $40 or $50 a day with not too much extra effort. Wouldn't it?

In the past, I've also applied my ice skating skills from high level hockey playing to teaching skating/hockey lessons. Two of the local ice rinks in our area allowed me to give private sessions on the condition that I also taught group classes for each once a week. I set my own pricing and taught three players simultaneously.

Ice hockey is an expensive sport and parents will pay quite a lot for the best for their kids. I was always paid on time for private lessons, and in cash. Many times I earned tips. The interaction with the kids and parents was always pleasant.

And lastly, although I didn't always enjoy it, for extra cash I would sometimes use my pick-up truck for hauling services. I worked for a moving company in college and have been asked to put that labor skill to use many times since.

My truck was 2WD, gets great mileage and is very dependable. I drove it every day. It was a resource that I own that helps me carry my equipment and boats around for one business while leaving opportunity to fill in the gaps or have a side stream in hauling services too.

This is real world, in person, labor that has paid off frequently. And something I could do at nearly any time if needed. People accumulate junk continuously. Later, I focused more on small- to medium-sized loads to be hauled in dump runs. Sometimes I'd pick up and move large pieces of furniture for family or friends in my network.

Finally, progressing in efficiency, I'd sub-contract out the work and broker the service myself. This saved me time and effort. The hard part is having a reliable service provider to work with the clients to whom I sell. While true of any business, it is especially so with this type of work. I can market the service, connect the labor with the customer and have them perform the work. I bill the customer electronically and pay the service provider. There might be a bit less room in this model for profitable margins, but it beats lifting heavy things all day. It's just another service to arbitrate that I was already familiar with from a young age. There are services today that allowyou to easily pair customers with service providers rather than doing it manually like this. More on that later.

Work smarter, not harder, right? Don't paddle upstream, go with the flow; get in tune with your wavelength in the world. Listen to the internal cues that drive you to do what you enjoy. Convert them into revenue streams. Don't be too proud to roll up your sleeves every now and then too. Many fortunes have been made with less than glamorous work. Use your own personal power and energy to propel you towards what you want in life.

Today, my company owns equity positions in other companies and I provide marketing and operational services for them. Essentially my LLC owns portions of other LLC's. This is an added layer of liability protection for me and represents assets my company could sell at a later date. These are smaller, but promising companies that I've "invested" some sweat equity in that needed my strengths to continue to thrive. Truthfully, I already have most of the systems in place these companies need so it isn't too much up front work on my part. These are my companies now, but I intend to use them as investments in the near future or the long run.

Self-Reflection Questions and Actions

1. **List any ideas you gleaned from Chris' scenario.**

2. **Reflect on the different types of work Chris performs. How could pride block you from working creatively like Chris?**

3. **List 2 actions you can take to implement any new ideas learned from this chapter.**

6 YOU CAN DO THIS TOO

Think about what you've amassed in skill or equipment during your life. Make a list of all those things available to you. What can you put to use for a potential income stream? Take note of all your skills and the things you own or can rent. Focus on two, three, or even four pursuits. With any of the services Chris can offer he can earn $60 per hour or more in his local area. So if one of these areas takes a hit or he can't or doesn't want to do it anymore, the other streams can pick up the slack. Diversification; just like the investments in your portfolio, it now underpins your career. Reclaim power and increase the ownership in what you produce.

First, be clear. Use the right mentality. Opportunities, resources, deals, and money exist in abundance. We must condition ourselves to see the opportunities so we can connect the dots and put together lucrative transactions. Typically, people think money and wealth are scarce. That's partially true, but often it's our own fears holding us back from harvesting what exists in abundance. What makes things more valuable? Their scarcity. Jobs are scarce. People are waiting around for companies to benevolently bestow employment upon them. Wealth can take many forms and mean different things to different people. The same is true for the concept of value. What one person finds valuable, another may not. Value, like beauty, is in the mind of the beholder.

People with a scarcity attitude feel deprivation: a lack of jobs, lack of money, lack of opportunities. That kind of thinking leads to resentment of other people or groups. Scarcity-thinkers want to take rather than give or create because they fear there's not enough for everyone. Do you want to be a giver, or a taker?

People with an attitude of wealth see opportunities and resources everywhere. They see a wealth of deals to be made, relationships to develop, and resources of which to take advantage. They are givers. Their kind of thinking can liberate minds from the confines of an attitude of scarcity. An attitude of wealth doesn't foster resentment of others. It opens doors and possibilities. Try to foster this attitude in yourself.

Thinking in terms of wealth versus scarcity is an attitude that develops with time and practice. After years of being "taught" that we should sacrifice for others, that we should not be selfish, it's hard to break those old thoughts.

Opportunities are limitless. There are always deals to be made. Rewire your brain to see them, not wait around for someone else to give you a small piece after the fact. Manage the power!

People often think money comes from:

1. Their boss (the company).
2. Rich people.
3. The government.

It actually comes from *assets and customers*. I know earlier we said the government controls the money supply and that is true, but they usually aren't paying it directly to most of us. Unless you realize this, you may be tempted to sit back and wonder why people higher up the corporate ladder or in government aren't giving you more of it. You've done a good job, of course you deserve it. But, will they even notice? You have to take it from the customers, your own customers, yourself. And you need to buy assets that pay you going forward.

Scarcity can be good in a specialized, hard-to-come-by skill, but as far as money, value, and "wealth" are concerned, there is more than enough to go around. The most valuable commodity in the universe is information and/or the knowledge that comes with learning that information. Don't feel guilty or have hang ups about being successful or propelling yourself forward.

Always have a side job/side stream project. Ideally, have more than one. Why? If you have a side stream, you acquire a quiet sense of confidence, smiling inwardly with the knowledge that if an employer ever dumps you, you have a safety net.

Begin by finding another source of regular income – a "tributary" flowing into your primary stream. Start with something that pays based on single transactions then look for recurring revenue models.

An example of a single transaction is a project for which you are paid when finished. You consult for a finite period for which you are paid on completion, or when delivered.

A recurring revenue model is a subscription to your services. Customers will pay you X amount of dollars per month in exchange for an ongoing service. It might be for a specified length of time like six or 12 months. Or it might be open-ended, until the client tells you to stop.

It could also be in the form of income from rental properties. This is a good example of passive income, in which the service is provided without your presence being necessary. Service in person is active income. The eventual goal, for the more sophisticated, would be to amass more of the passive income streams that would feed your account while you move on to other things. Even this book for me serves as a small piece of my overall strategy for relatively passive income streams.

Diversify the streams of income. Add another side stream that does not induce conflict but instead diversifies the income in a complementary manner. One stream may help you build or feed off of another. Build a work life with components that are complementary. If you're a ski instructor, you cannot do it year round. You need to find something else that is complementary in the summer season.

An example of conflicting streams would be a situation in which a personal trainer who needs to see clients before and after the work day, obtains a real estate license. Many potential property clients also want to meet at night. This conflicts with the personal training clients: unrelated but conflicting streams.

Tax season is mostly four months of the year. If you become an accountant, you might spend much of the rest of the year bookkeeping or strategic planning: related and complementary streams. Or, the streams could be non-conflicting and unrelated.

Apart from a good learning attitude the most important assets are the people with whom you keep company.

Remember, you are the sum of the five people with whom you spend the most time!

Imagine that you tell your five beer-drinking poker buddies that you want to venture on your own and make a fortune. What would they tell you? They would laugh their socks off before tearing your ego into a million pieces.

People are often jealous. Some don't want to see the people around them succeed. If you succeed, it makes them look bad. They know in their hearts that they are going nowhere yet they embrace that attitude and pull you down with them. They will steal your dream, and rob you of your financial freedom if you are not careful!

It's the crab mentality. Any one crab could climb up out of the fisherman's bucket and escape, but the others will always grab hold and drag him back to their level. They will self-police to the point that none of them can escape the predicament in which they find themselves.

The key point: mix with positive minded people. Positive thinking is not wishful thinking. A wishful thinker is a dreamer who doesn't take action. Positive thinking is backed by action. You will feel the energy of people who believe in you and support your dreams.

If you hang out with ducks, you will quack … but if you hang out with eagles, you will soar!

Fill yourself with positive information. Associate with positive people. Fill your mind with inspiring material. Don't spend time chatting about negatives that bring people down. Get rid of that negative energy. People avoid negativity. Look for people who follow your vision or are willing to grow with you.

Lastly, you must BELIEVE IN YOURSELF! Stepping out of your comfort zone may seem terrifying. Many will not support your dream and they will go on the offensive. It could be your parents or your spouse.

You may be faced with the question: is my financial freedom worth the price I am paying? Can I live another day with the same routine, the same job, the same pay check or the same drudgery? If the answer is no, then take action NOW, not tomorrow, or you could forget your dream.

Write your desire on a piece of paper and hang on tight every day. Share it with someone positive and take that first step.

Self-Reflection Questions and Actions

1. **You are the sum of the five people with whom you spend the most time. List the 5 most positive people you know. What qualities do they have that you admire?**

2. **List at least one substantive thing each of those 5 positive individuals GIVES you. Do you GIVE anything in return?**

3. **Make a list, write the qualities you wish to ADOPT from your 5 most positive friends. Post this list where you can see it and view it regularly.**

4. **Make a list, write what you can GIVE to others. This list where you can see it. Focus on being a giver, not a taker. It will create a positive flow of energy and goodwill.**

7 GET STARTED TODAY

Follow these simple initial steps.

- Find something you are interested in and create one new side stream of revenue.

- Start small and add pieces, or streams. Single jobs, projects, or transactions are likely to take place first. Then look for repeat business or recurring revenue models.

- Give up streams that become outdated, unproductive, or burdensome. Know when to cut your losses and walk away.

Must Do's

If you're going to start a legitimate business, as opposed to a side stream of revenue or operating as a sole proprietor, here are some steps to getting up and running in the United States.

Incorporation: Make sure to incorporate with your state corporation commission or equivalent office. Check with your attorney or accountant to be sure. Obtain a local county or town business license.

Call the IRS and obtain an EIN (employer identification number). This is like your business' social security number. You'll need it to open your business bank account later. Be sure to obtain any trademarks, either state or national, that might be pertinent to your business logo and/or slogan.

Name Your Business: Name your business something that describes what you do or offer and which reflects your personal brand. The same applies to your logo design. To operate under a different business name or a shortened name you can file a simple DBA – Doing Business As – form with your state corporation commission. This may apply if you don't want to use the LLC at the end of your name should you chose to incorporate as a limited liability company.

Taxes: Consult with your accountant and set up all necessary federal and state tax accounts. Some accountants will come in one day per week and take care of your transactions for the week in one shot. Better yet, they can monitor your transactions and work with you virtually. Sometimes you can find a personal assistant or concierge who can do your bookkeeping. If you have employees, further accounts need to be set up. Pay your estimated taxes on a quarterly basis as that may be the most economical. Taxation for this type of entity (LLC) is what is called pass through. You still pay your taxes on income you took out of this entity just as you would on any other earned income. You may NOT pay yourself a regular paycheck though where taxes are withheld out of each check. You take an owner's draw and pay taxes quarterly or annually as stated above.

Bank Account: Go to your favorite local bank (there is not much difference between them). Set up a business checking account, merchant services to accept credit cards and, most importantly, EFT (electronic funds transfer) or ARB (automatic recurring billing). Preferably go to a bank where you have a contact. Sometimes a local credit union can be a good option, and, in some instances, better than larger banks. See if you can set up a business line of credit at that same visit. It's a little extra cushion for the future. Based on our experience, credit unions may not be as good in dealing with small businesses as some of the commercial banks, but it's worth looking into first. The EIN number from the IRS will be necessary to set up your account.

You may not have much money to open the account. But you can use the revenue from the first client if necessary.

If you're really bootstrapping, you may be able to make early use of some online resources like Paypal™ or perhaps Google

Checkout. Paypal™ has a virtual terminal option and a subscription feature for recurring billing of clients. It also provides merchant services such as the web code for buttons you can simply cut and paste into your website as you develop it.

Legal Advice: If you can afford it, find an attorney and pay him a retainer to become your adviser when legal issues arise. At the very least, create a list of people you could call. Additionally, some services like Pre-paid Legal or even Legal Zoom, can offer some peace of mind and help solve small or routine legal issues.

Insurance: You may need personal liability and business insurance. Check with a local independent insurance agent. Alternatively, your bank might offer one of these programs. If you operate as a sole proprietor or a consultant, use the sample consultant agreement provided (see Appendix).

Self-Reflection Questions and Actions

1. **What did you learn from this chapter?**

2. **What resources do you need to get started? Using the chapter as a resource, list them.**

3. **Identify at least 2 actions you can take to move forward.**

8 THE REWARDS

You can make your own schedule and work when you are most productive. If I sit down and try to work straight through a full work day, I have trouble, particularly if looking at a computer screen for long periods. It's hard on both my eyes, and my brain concentrating on multiple tasks simultaneously. I need periodic breaks so I can maintain focus. Have you noticed that your best ideas come in the shower or while driving in your car, but you can't summon them when sitting at the work computer?

I know my body's rhythms and I am not energetic throughout the entire day. My most productive times are between 6 and 8 am while around 10.30 am is a good time to stop for a quick snack. I have a serious energy and mental acuity crash around 2 to 3 pm. A power nap is not out of the question. Many times, I'll keep my laptop with me on the couch after dinner while I watch TV for several hours between about 7 and 11 pm. This is a good time to connect with friends and others on social media. At the same time I have good ideas reading other material and may get a burst of productivity then too. If nothing else, I have ideas for the next day. My productivity isn't in one giant, solid block of time. Likely, yours isn't either. Recognize that and make the most of your best times.

You don't have to feel uncomfortable working for someone else. I just never felt comfortable doing it. I really don't like too much team work and it's much better for me to direct myself. That's not true for everyone, but most of us, deep down, have more desire than we think to pursue our own interests. Or, if I want to take advantage of one of my down times to save energy for a more productive period, I can do that.

You make the rules. You only answer to customers. That's an important point. Whether you make yourself your own boss or not, you're still there to serve someone else and make their life better in some way.

Concentrate on the parts of the job you are most interested in or passionate about. Outsource the rest. It's true that entrepreneurs often end up doing everything many times. You may *need* to do that initially, but not forever. I don't mind attending business functions but I don't like bookkeeping or solving IT problems. Otherwise, I've performed every function imaginable. The bottom line is what counts. The "high" from closing a big deal is what really gets me excited. I prefer to focus on that side of my business if I can; the most revenue-producing functions.

Connect directly to customers and take ownership of your work. This is what keeps you passionate, full of pride, and not part of the "working dead." In a highly specialized job for a large company, you may never see or get to know a customer. What incentives are in place for you to care about the customer or the quality of the product or service they receive?

Not much, right? Developing relationships with customers, and having their feedback can help keep all of that in the forefront and become part of the reward for the work you have done.

Working for yourself enables you to see the direct relationship between your efforts and monetary reward. Pay yourself for your actual production and performance. It's like digging for gold. If you know you dig a little bit and you get a little gold, it motivates you to work harder and dig deeper. It more clearly associates the reward (whether monetary or otherwise) with the actual work performed.

Job security is only an illusion. Don't allow yourself to be pulled into a situation that is not ideal simply because there is an illusion of security. You can still take steps to secure yourself and your income. A good start is to not put all your eggs into one basket.

You will no longer need to rely on one employer. Diversifying my income streams has made me less dependent on any one potential employer. Manage the power well. Don't give employers influence over aspects of your life.

Do not depend on the government. As I don't want to depend on any one employer, nor do I want to put the incomes of other Americans in jeopardy either. We must recognize that everything we get from the government is something that is taken from someone else.

You will not be a burden on others. Make use of relationships with friends, family, and connections. Try to enhance their lives, as well as those of your customers. Don't be afraid to ask for help, but also realize that it is reciprocal. Be a giver.

Things are not always as they seem. We should not do things simply because "that's the way it's always been done." Be open and accepting of change. Many people aren't aware of other options – like different forms of affordable health insurance, for example. If you learn new ways to achieve your goals, share your knowledge. It may also create an opportunity to build relationships within your chosen industry.

Self-Reflection Questions and Actions

1. **What did you learn from Chris in this chapter that you can apply to your own life?**

2. **List at least 2 actions you can take to help yourself move forward.**

9 SUCCESSFUL CONSULTING

Freelancing and Consulting

When you think of a freelancer, what is the first thing that comes to mind? You may think of a writer, novelist or journalist. You may have heard of freelance photographers. What about freelance software designers, freelance medical billing specialists, or even freelance scientific researchers?

These are jobs that have experienced massive growth in recent years as more and more people realize they can make far more money working as freelancers than they can working solely for their previous employer.

It sounds pretty good, doesn't it? You work in a field of expertise for quite a few years, gain practical experience then gradually make the switch from the full working day to becoming your own boss as a freelancer or consultant.

Is it really as easy as it sounds? Keep in mind there are quite a few freelancers who only work part time. This is not because they make a ton of money and need only work a couple of days per week. It's because they had trouble finding work in the past and needed a better career option. So here, freelancing or consulting is merely one stream for them.

However, this scenario need not apply to you if you are willing to do whatever it takes to become a freelancer. Eventually, you can become highly successful at what you do in this stream.

The first step in making that jump from an office to freelancing is deciding whether or not you have what it takes.

We all want to be our own boss, but do all of us possess the drive and dedication it can take to be successful without the watchful eye of a supervisor? Sadly, we don't. Therefore, you have to think about what makes you special in a world of freelancers or consultants.

To start raking in the cash later you need to be willing to start off slowly along your new freelance path.

Don't quit your job just yet! Instead, hunt for freelance work in your area of expertise on the internet with some informal market research.

Some skills, including the ability to write coherently or undertake software design for any type of client, are highly marketable.

Conversely, if you are only able to do tasks that are easily marketable, you may have a harder time finding work for a freelance operation.

Some of the most popular fields for consulting include writing, editing, photography, web and graphic design, software design, and architecture or drafting.

Once you have chosen your freelance field you need your first clients. Do not, however, start with any clients connected to your current job. Various laws prohibit what can effectively amount to stealing clients.

Instead, turn to your favorite search engine and hunt through forums and databases specifically designed for freelancers seeking work in a particular field. Ask your friends and family.

There are tons of different sites available that within about an hour may have yielded at least 10 bookmarks for potential employment as a freelancer.

With any free time, you can search each of your bookmarked websites to find the best-sounding freelance positions.

Initially, you may need to take a few low-paying jobs. They are useful in helping build your skill set as well as your portfolio and testimonials of your work.

They will also help you learn how to better manage your time, speed up your workflow, and help with internet-based research for projects.

The low-paying jobs will no doubt continue until you have assembled a massive list of satisfied clients. They will help you compete with other freelancers in your field in tandem with your low your rates and fees.

Eventually you will graduate into higher paying jobs and with it the realization that consulting or freelancing has significantly increased your income. Don't be too proud to start at the bottom and work your way up in life.

Pros and Cons

Working for yourself on a per client basis has both benefits and drawbacks that you need to research before you start.

Many people will tell you that leaving an office environment was the best thing they ever did. Others could not wait for each freelance project to end because they hated the stress of their assignments.

Here are some of the most common benefits and drawbacks you will face.

Benefits

The moment you decide to become a freelancer, you may be told how "cool" it is to be your own boss. You are in control of your work and nobody else (except your clients) can tell you what to do. If you don't want to work on Fridays you don't have to. Take any days off you want, but you must finish your projects by the deadline.

As your own boss, you have freedom to steer your life where you want it to go. You can plan your own schedules, choose the projects that you find enjoyable, charge any rate you please, and be almost totally self-sufficient.

Another big benefit of freelancing and consulting is that you can set your own dress code. If you find all your freelance work online, who is to say that you can't hang around in your pajamas or underwear all day? There is no sense in getting dressed up when you can just get out of bed, enjoy a cup of hot coffee and plop yourself down at the computer to start work. Consulting creates the opportunity to work in your own style and in total comfort.

A freelancer can potentially spend a lot more time with family and friends because there is no need to work on a strict office schedule. Spend time with your children when they get home from school, drive them to play dates or activities, meet your friends or have a date with your spouse whenever they are free.

The flexibility of a freelance income stream is second to none. There is practically no other job in the world that gives you both the spare time and the financial freedom to do what you want, when you want.

Finally, consulting has a near limitless income potential. Working for yourself means you can keep all of what you earn. Not a penny goes to anyone else (apart from taxes and living expenses).

All profit belong to you but remember will likely need to re-invest a portion of it into your business to continue the hunt for clients. Further, because you work on a per project basis, you can accept as many projects as you want to earn as much money as you wish.

You are not salaried, so the more work you do, the more you get paid. This alone puts you directly in touch with the rewards from your work, unlike a specialized, salaried job. This can wake you from the zombie-like state of the "working dead."

Drawbacks

There are a few. First, you are not as financially stable as a salaried employee. You need to manage your money yourself and ensure a stream of projects to make enough money to stay afloat financially. You must constantly market yourself for future work. In some countries, such as the United States, you have to provide for your own healthcare. These three factors create a feeling of fiscal insecurity for many people, and a deterrent because of the major financial risk involved.

There is also heavy competition in the world of freelancing. The internet has been both a blessing and a curse. On the one hand it has opened doors and made the world of consulting more accessible to anyone who has contemplated self-employment. On the other hand, the internet has increased competition for clients among freelancers and forced start-ups to offer very low rates for initial jobs.

Self-Reflection Questions and Actions

1. **Do you have a large enough skill set to enable you to stand out among the hordes of different people seeking the same work? Refer to your skills inventory you conducted earlier in this workbook.**

2. **Do you have the time management skills necessary to run your own consulting operation and meet all deadlines set by your clients in the absence of your familiar structured work environment?**

3. **List at least 2 actions you can take to move forward.**

10 HOW TO GET INTO THE FREELANCING OR CONSULTING BUSINESS

We have all read an article, seen a photograph, tinkered with some software, or visited a website that was designed by some type of freelancer. At some point we have all contemplated leaving our specialized jobs in large offices and starting afresh – alone. But, why don't we?

What holds so many of us back? Why do we allow ourselves to be tied to our employer as if some invisible shackles enslave us? What types of skills do we need to break free from typical nine to five shifts? All these questions need to be asked first.

Too many people quit their jobs to pursue freelance careers only to fail and crawl back to their previous employer for their job.

This unfortunate circumstance happens for one reason: the prospective freelancer had no idea what to expect. He was told he could be free, have as many days off as he wanted and retain all the profits from his work.

But nobody told him that he also may have to work long and hard to meet deadlines, manage his finances himself, and compete with thousands of others for the same clients.

It takes a special kind of person to work 60 hours a week for himself or herself so they don't have to work 40 hours a week for someone else.

Before venturing into this world, know that it is not all fun and games. Lots of serious thought must go into your actions if you are to be successful. Having thought it over and feeling sure that freelancing or consulting is right for you, it is time to start looking for work. Be absolutely certain not to violate any agreements you might have with a current employer.

Do not quit your job right away as you will not have a livable source of income for a few months, at least, while searching for paying projects.

A first step should be to log onto your computer, pull open your web browser of choice, head over to one of the top three search engines, and start looking.

Use specific keywords to describe what you want and you should wind up with a massive database of different websites that cater to the freelance community in your field.

Once you have constructed a list of the top websites where clients are likely to be found visit the sites daily (or subscribe to them) to find projects that would not only be interesting but pay the bills.

As time passes, and you amass clients, more and more people will hear of you and the kind of work you do.

In this way you can attract the higher paying projects that will really supplement your income.

Eventually potential clients may come to you because of your good reputation. Word of mouth referrals are one of the most powerful marketing tools available.

It's important to create a collection of different items that can showcase your work. A portfolio may be critical to your success as a freelancer.

Include only the projects for which you retain full rights. If word gets around that someone thinks you may have stolen pieces of their portfolio, you risk damaging your reputation beyond repair. People will not work with you. And never, ever plagiarize even one single word. Always give credit to the original source. Always work with integrity and respect for the efforts of others.

Imagine are looking for freelance work as a web designer. You *could* include an article you wrote on chemistry. But, why would someone looking for a skilled web designer care about something you wrote for a chemistry website, unless your client was also hiring you to write his web copy?

Finally, competition from around the globe is another barrier to self-sufficiency. Prepare to offer something that the competition simply cannot compete with and at much lower price points.

For example, noting a native tongue, such as English or French, for a freelance writer or editor, can be a plus. Ease of communication could be a big selling point for clients in many countries.

Graphic and web designers as well as software programmers should take plenty of extra courses, both in and out of college to illustrate how well they are educated in their craft.

Finally, no matter what your field take the time to create additions to your portfolio that highlight your strong points.

For more on how to conduct competitive analysis, let's look at what our friends from www.industry-templates.com say:

"Competitive Research Framework

First, determine how you define your direct competition and indirect competition. What kinds of companies would qualify as competitors? If you are already aware of some market players, write those company names down. Next, jot down a list of the key phrases an end customer would use to search for your product or service. Example: For my new business, (providing "done for you" business templates and worksheets for a number of industries), a good *direct* search term is "web development business templates" or for *indirect*, "business templates" (A bad (not properly targeted) phrase is "web development templates." In a web search, the absence of the word "business" results in graphical and HTML *web site design* templates – which is not at all what I'm selling.) Use your list of 5-10 key phrases to find websites for competing businesses.

Once you've established a hearty a list of competitors (and determined each is indeed a competitor), it's time to learn more about each. Start by compiling a standard set of information about each company.

For each company, research and record the following information:

1. Company Name

2. URL (www.companyname.com)

3. Competitor Type (Direct or Indirect?)

4. Company Opening Year

    A. Check the website's "about us" page, check incorporation filing records, or alternatively, when the domain was first registered.

    B. If they have a Facebook company page, this info is likely available in the timeline feature.

5. List of Products or Services (including Pricing)

6. Ranking

    A. How closely to watch this business.

    B. Ex: 3 = "Regularly", 2 = "Periodically", 1 = "Seldomly"

7. Any other info you are specifically interested in.

    A. Examples: What kinds of customer support do they provide? What feeling does the website give the end customer? What writing style is used to communicate with the end customer? Etc, etc, etc.

For each website, take a screenshot of the home page, and other pages that contain information you might want to reference later. (Website content changes all the time. Don't assume the content you were interested in will be there next time you visit!)

Now that you have the basic information, it's time to dig deeper. There are a number of ways to learn more about your competition.

Again, the best way really is to introduce yourself. You'll learn and gain more from forming a business relationship, rather than just "mystery shopping" them. Set the tone properly in the beginning by making it clear that you are in a similar industry. Be upfront that you are researching the industry and are interested in starting a business. Network with them, visit their booth at industry event, or reach out via LinkedIn or a similar industry network. Ask them for an information interview where you can learn more about them and their business. Find out what they look for in a partner. (That partner could be you in the future!) If you have the opportunity, talk with their customers or suppliers. Hire them or buy one of their products. (There is a lot to learn from experiencing their purchasing and fulfillment process.) Ultimately, you want to get a sense of their strengths and weaknesses, their competitive advantages over their competition, and any key brand differentiators.

Other Online Research Tools and Methods

There are a number of free ways or inexpensive tools to aid you in learning about competitors as well as keeping up with their successes over time. Here are a few:

- Subscribe to competitors' email newsletters (or RSS feed)
- Subscribe to Twitter feeds and pages on Facebook and LinkedIn
- Subscribe to keyword alerts
    - Get an email when certain phrases show up online. Three easy to use services are Google Alerts, Yahoo Alerts, and Twilert (for Twitter).

Online information sources and miscellaneous tools. (Enter your competitor's site and compare it to your own!)

- Social Mention – Search posts, videos, and online mentions for a brand. (Also create brand keyword alerts.)

- [Wikipedia](#) – Look for competitor informational pages.

- [Compete.com](#), [Alexa](#), [Quantcast](#) – Website analytics, audience, and site traffic analysis.

- [Hoovers](#), [Dun & Bradstreet](#) – Search global business records and information.

- [NameChk](#) – Check a username or vanity url at dozens of popular Social Networking and Social Bookmarking websites. (i.e.: See what social networks competitors are using. Also check to see if your "brand username" is available.)

- [Google Trends](#) – Compare search traffic for two topics. (Ex: Type "Coke, Pepsi" to compare one soda company against the other.)

- [Wappalyzer](#) – A browser extension that uncovers technologies used on websites. Detects what content management systems, web shops, and other online tools your competitors are using.

- [KeywordSpy](#), [SpyFu](#) – Insite into a website's keywords and ad spending.

Please note: While some of the tools above touch on keywords and online search, the intent at this stage is less about SEO (search engine optimization) and more about getting acquainted with competition websites. (SEO research is a sizeable topic for another day.)

Put How to Conduct Competitive Research to Use:

1. Determine what kinds of companies would qualify as your direct or indirect competition. Make a list of any company names you're already aware of.

2. Create a list of key phrases an end customer would use to search for your product or service. Use this list and a

search engine to uncover additional competitors.

3. Research each company individually, compiling a standard set of comparative information."

Reference: http://www.industry-templates.com/blog/business-formation/online-competitive-research/

Self-Reflection Questions and Actions

1. **After reading this chapter, what are the positive things your resume and/or portfolio offer prospective clients and/or partners?**

2. **What do you need to improve/change to attract clients and/or partners?**

3. **List your top 3 potential competitors in your market space.**

4. **List at least 2 actions you can take to move forward.**

11 WHERE TO LOOK FOR MULTIPLE CUSTOMERS

Not so long ago the best route for a freelancer to a potentially high paying client was solely through residents and local businesses in the community.

It was easier for writers, rather than web designers or software programmers, due to the large number of magazines and newspapers that traditionally needed constant freelance contributions.

Thanks to the Internet, finding work has never been easier. Individuals and companies always need freelancers for a project or two. They can help you get started and hopefully you might be lucky enough to find a client that wants to work with you time and time again.

A freelancer can also use the internet to market services on various forums and other freelance websites. In this way prospective clients come to you while you work on other projects.

Promoting yourself is an important first step. Let everyone know who you are, what you do, how well you do it, and how to contact you.

Potential clients love a freelancer who is willing to get the job done right the first time and fast. Finding clients in masses requires targeting various forums and discussion boards that dot the web.

Using Google is a great way to search for different websites that are specific to your chosen freelance field. Don't post advertisements on forums not frequented by people in your line of work. Posting out of section could result in you being banned.

Because it is important to focus on freelance websites directed to your field of operation, chose one or two services where you might find freelance work and go from there.

It is much easier to find work online as a writer, editor, photographer, web designer, or software programmer because there are many different freelance directories available.

One of the best places to start – for any type of freelancer – is craigslist, www.craigslist.com. This is a one-stop shop that lists jobs, both full-time and part-time "gigs", in metropolitan areas as well as in cities and countries. Most of the jobs offered on craigslist allow remote working from home although visits to offices in some of the higher paying positions may be necessary occasionally.

Additionally, build a list of potential customers using Fiverr, at www.fiverr.com. It's a site where people offer nearly anything for a mere $5. For example, one advertisement in the writing and editing category began with this title: *I will proofread your college essay for grammar and spelling up to 1,000 words.* Another stated this: *I will proofread any 2000 word text in Romanian for $5.* Yet another offered: *I will proofread and edit up to 500 words for $5.* Which freelancer would you choose?

Smaller jobs may help gain the trust of customers who return for repeat business. Another amazing resource for freelancers of all kinds is Guru, www.guru.com, a website that helps freelancers in all fields find customers from around the world. It caters mostly to established freelance professionals though, so you may want to turn to it once you have exhausted other consulting options.

There are several excellent consulting websites for freelance writers and editors. One of them is Freelance Writing: www.freelancewriting.com. This is a massive database where employers and freelancers post information to find suitable matches for individual projects. Although catering to mostly lower paying jobs, it is a great start for your first consult or if you are looking simply for part-time projects to supplement your current income. As one of the leading websites also for those involved in programming and design, it is probably the most likely place to find a well paid job in the web and software field.

Among other website resource options is Freelance Job Search, www.freelancejobsearch.com a website that posts lesser known, but better paying freelance jobs in web design, graphic design, and programming. Designers and programmers could also turn to Script Lance, now www.freelancer.com, as a source of new leads.

The Writer's Market, www.writersmarket.com is also a site, not only to find work but to check out the writing and editing business. Get in touch with potential clients as well as hone your skills.

Another new resource has just launched. Power To Fly is a new career service that matches home-based workers with employers. See www.powertofly.com.

These resources are a great start in your freelancing or consulting efforts. Pretty soon by working for yourself and diversifying your income, you'll be more connected and passionate about your work as well as less dependent on any one person or organization.

Self-Reflection Questions and Actions

1. **What resources can you use from this chapter to find work? Highlight them for future reference.**

2. **What resources do not apply to you from this chapter?**

3. **List at least 2 actions you can take to move forward.**

12 WORKING AT HOME? TIME IS OF THE ESSENCE!

The main reason some say they want to work at home is because they work only when they want to work. It *is* true that you can set your own work hours at home but it does *not* mean that you don't need set work hours. More than likely, at some point, you'll be at the mercy of a client's schedule among other things.

A 'hit or miss' work schedule – a lack of any work schedule at all – simply will not work. Time is of the Essence! YOUR time!

Working at home can be a very, very good thing. You see the kids off to school and are there when they get home. You can put on a load of laundry and work while it runs through the cycles. You can schedule medical, dental and other appointments or pick up kids from day camps during vacations. Dinner can be cooked well before a flock of hungry buzzards descends.

It can also be a very, very bad thing if you can't plan your time well or don't set up a work schedule in which you and your family can operate. When you work at home, despite the automatic perks, time management is essential.

Inefficiency – spending too much time accomplishing tasks – could lead to failure on the work or home front. Not only must you establish a work schedule, it needs to be enforced you, your family and friends as well. Many women, in particular, who work from home are often interrupted with phone calls from family members when they need to be working.

A job in the brick and mortar world provides:

1. Structure for your day.

2. A signal to family and friends that your time is spoken for during working hours.

Notice that both these benefits provided by a regular job relate to your TIME.

First, let's discuss the structure a regular job provides and how it can be applied to your work-at-home job or business. A job outside the home requires your presence during a specified time on specified days of the week. Working from home needs the same kind of structure, in particular a set number of regular working hours. You can choose the hours … but you do have to choose!

Now, let's talk about your family and friends and how they view your work-at-home job. It is a strange but true fact that your dear mother would not *dream* of calling you at your 'real' job to ask you to drive Aunt Rosie to the beauty salon and wait until she is finished. After all, you are *working* and can't be expected to leave your job to run errands. Right?

That very same considerate mother *will* call and ask you to transport Aunt Rosie to and from the salon when you work from home. Why? Because you are at home and available.

Your mother will not view your work-at-home job as a 'real' job. Your spouse will see you as being free to run errands. And friends will want you to be available for long telephone conversations, lunch, or for a coffee klatch. Nobody will understand why you are sitting on the couch with your laptop, wearing your pajamas or underwear.

You can see the problem. If you do not schedule your time and abide by your schedule yourself, others will not. Unless you see your work-at-home job as a *real* job with *real* working hours, your time will be eaten up. You will not be able to finish anything.

You will fail and find yourself looking for a *real* job unless you view your work at home job as the *real* thing with regular working hours that make you unavailable for other activities.

The best way to accomplish this is to set a schedule and inform your family and friends what it is. You don't have to be rude but you do have to be firm. Make it clear to all. Pin up a note.

"I will be working between 9 am and 3 pm Monday through Friday. On those days and during those hours, I am not available to run errands or take personal phone calls or entertain company." Then stick to it!

For work-at-home entrepreneurs time is their single most valuable asset. Nothing can replace time – valuable, precious time!

No matter how rich or poor you are, no matter how many things are on your 'to-do' list, there are still only 24 hours in each day.

But we can't spend all of them working. We have to sleep, eat and shower. Family and friends also require some of our time. Relationships must be nurtured, not neglected. We can allow ourselves just so many work hours each day. Since our working time is limited that means we must make the very most of the hours we work. We can't waste time on unimportant details or on tasks that others can do.

When you shave a few minutes from your schedule, you will make more efficient use of your allotted work hours. Here are a few suggestions.

Email Account Efficiency

We all have various email accounts. One is for this and another is for that. Checking every email account more than once a day can be time-consuming but shortened by having all email delivered into one gmail account. Additionally, don't spend time reading and answering emails that don't add to your bottom line.

Email comes in several varieties. There are emails that are business-related, emails that are important but not business-related and emails that are simply frivolous and time wasting. If an email has been forwarded several times, don't waste your time.

If an email is addressed to a great many people, don't waste time on it either. Email can consume a lot of time. You need to filter the important from the irrelevant and only spend time on those emails that are related to your business.

Set Up Time Tables to Help Prioritize Your Work Day

A scheduled work day is an efficient work day. You will accomplish more in less time if you know in advance, and can see at a glance, what task is next. A timetable is a visual aid. It can help you allot your time efficiently and productively.

Focus on Result-Producing Activities

When you make your work day schedule, be certain that the tasks will, in fact, make your business thrive. Don't waste time, effort and energy on tasks that can be done by others. Investigate outsourcing and add hours to your day by sending mundane business tasks to others.

You can outsource bookkeeping and accounting, article and ebook submissions, travel and event planning and ad writing. Others may be able to perform these tasks better and more efficiently. Your time is better spent growing your business, making those contacts and closing those deals!

Shave Time on Counter-Productive Activities

Your friends and families demand some of your time but you can also waste a lot on unproductive activities like watching TV. Keep a record of what you do over several days and you'll be surprised at how much of your day is wasted.

Of course, we all need down time. We must relax our minds and bodies. We can't be all business all the time, but we can limit our unproductive or counterproductive activities. Time is precious and limited. We need to make the best use of every minute.

Outsourcing: How to Get More Done in Less Time

Time equals money. You are an entrepreneur. Ask yourself about the best use of your time because it is *your* time that equals money.

The health of your bottom line is directly affected by the way you choose to allot your working hours.

Your job as an entrepreneur is to grow your business, to make those contacts that will make you money. Your job is to conceive ideas and bring them to fruition. Your job is to close that deal!

Okay! Now for what your job as an entrepreneur is not. It does not qualify you as an accountant, an advertising guru or a writer. You aren't qualified to be an event planner or a travel agent. When you decided to build a career and become an entrepreneur it did not automatically make you a "jack-of-all-trades."

You can waste a lot of valuable time on tasks that you aren't very good at. You are the idea man/woman. You'll be good at making your business grow if that is where you use your time and direct your energies.

Doing it all yourself, whether you are good at it or not, will use up all thought and energy leaving nothing for what only you can do to make your business grow. The 80/20 rule is likely to be at work here too. Remember to focus only on the 20 per cent that brings you the most revenue and outsource the rest or as much as you can.

Accountant or Bookkeeping Service

Every business must keep a record of its day-to-day financial transactions. The smallest of transactions can add up to big tax deductions over a year. You can't simply file everything under 'miscellaneous' spend even an hour every day attending to mundane bookkeeping duties either. Bookkeepers and accountants charge only for the time that they spend working for you. Usually they have many clients. It's easy to make use of their services. In fact, some never meet their bookkeepers because they work completely virtually.

If a bookkeeper spends an hour working on your records then you will charged for that one hour. You aren't a bookkeeper or an accountant so you may spend three or four hours on the same tasks, with questionable results. Hire an accountant or a bookkeeping service – particularly if they charge $40 per hour and you can make $60 per hour doing what you do best. It's a no-brainer.

One of my favorite new resources is now a Go Daddy product. An automated small business bookkeeping service for $10/month. Go to www.outright.com to see how it works. It's simple and automatically pulls in all of your online banking transactions and categorizes them for you.

Hire a VA (Virtual Assistant)

You don't have to do all of it yourself. You can scale up your venture by replicating yourself, hiring more people, or outsourcing tasks that do not produce much revenue. Virtual assistants are a great resource for your side business. They can work from anywhere in the world.

A great resource is http://www.onlinejobs.ph. It matches you with appropriate virtual assistant candidates. The pay rates are inexpensive for full-time virtual work. Many cost about $200-300 a *month*! They have a special section for pre-found, tested and scored professionals with their resumes compiled so that you can link with the right assistant.

Having others work virtually can bring financial advantages and allow you to make the most of your time. A virtual assistant can save hours of time on mundane tasks that are necessary for a successful business. They can check and filter your emails so only the most vital need your response. Internet entrepreneurs get more junk mail than anybody! A good VA can also act as a travel agent and book airline and hotel reservations.

Ghost Writers and Article Submission Services

Ghost writers will post to blogs and forums above your own signature file that includes your name and website. Some ghost writers will also submit articles and ebooks for you. If the ghost writer that you employ does not, then seek an articles submission company for that time-consuming task.

Advertising Agencies

These are not cheap so be specific about what you need. You may get pay per click advertisements written rather reasonably –a huge timesaver.

Self-Reflection Questions and Actions

1. **What can you do to set boundaries in the home environment to ensure that others in your household respect your work life?**

2. **What can you do in the home environment to effectively manage and protect your time?**

3. **List at least 2 actions you can implement to move forward.**

13 HOW TO SAVE MONEY, DEAL WITH CASH CRISES, AND SPEND LESS THAN COMPETITORS

The formula for determining profit on which budgets are based is **Income – Expenses = Profit.**

It isn't complicated and you don't need to be a rocket scientist to figure out that there are two ways to improve your profit.

1. Increase income

or

2. Decrease expenses

If you can figure out how to do both simultaneously, please let us know.

It would be nice to just crank up the burners and make more money, wouldn't it? Unfortunately increasing income is much harder than decreasing expenses when it comes to improving your bottom line.

At least once in a lifetime need is great and resources are few. This is particularly so if you make frequent transitions from one income stream to others. It can be hard enough to make ends meet on a decent wage with a single job. When times get tough and the money is not there to meet the need, a person can easily despair.

There is no magic formula for coming up with on-the-spot cash. But you can sleep better at night with good financial control and a plan of action should emergency funds be needed.

How to Cope in a Cash Crisis

Here's how to assess your situation and get back on your feet.

Without warning your roof begins to leak. Your hot water heater shuts down, your computer blows up, the clutch needs to be replaced and your son books his wedding on the Island of Oahu – in the same week! Oh, and your boss advises that a round of layoffs, that includes your job, is coming. Stunned and pondering an exit strategy a friendly letter arrives from the IRS explaining that you miscalculated your taxes in 1996, and your house is no longer your own. What do you do?

The above scenario looks like a financial emergency of biblical proportions. You can restore your financial life and equilibrium—and perhaps even fend off future misfortune—without having to sell your soul.

Money woes are usually accompanied by crippling emotional setbacks. This is particularly true of men who characteristically tie their self-worth to earning power. You will need to cope very well if you hope to make a solid financial comeback.

Whenever a money emergency hits, the ability of the individual to deal with huge amounts of stress that will keep things steady. Calm and rational study of each problem as it arises may lessen the feeling of being overwhelmed.

Calm must take center stage. You must *never* allow yourself the luxury of panic. No one is there to take over. It's just you. The more you panic, the less effective you will be. You need to keep a clear head to formulate an appropriate plan. Be aware of your own tendency to sabotage plans through panic. The first step in managing a money emergency is to remaining calm and optimistic. Don't act right away or you will inevitably make a mistake! Before you manage your finances again, you have to manage your emotions. Before you can begin your comeback plan you must regain your balance.

If your emergency demands quick action, think first about seeking advice from a debt counselor, money coach or financial planner. Whenever possible seek help from a financially-perceptive friend or family member.

Time to Crunch Some Numbers

The first step is to step back! Assess the damage. A big mistake often made in the throes of a financial crisis is failure to look clearly at the situation.

It is easy to be overwhelmed. However, totaling up the damage serves two important purposes. First, you need to know exactly how much you owe, how much money you have in hand and what it will take to cover the distance between the two. Second, you want to avoid other mishaps, such as penalties, further repairs, or missed deadlines.

If you are not properly prepared, you must prepare on the spot. Any type of money crisis creates a feeling of being cornered. It would be better to be prepared, but how likely is that?

Most people will be somewhat prepared. If the crisis is not too dire, they will be able to handle it. Others may be sunk from the start. Ideally, you would not be overwhelmed because you have a good plan of action, no matter how small. Unexpected expenses could be covered by funds in the irregular expenses of any good budget. Unfortunately, your emergency stash may not be enough. You would not be alone in this.

About this time you might turn to credit cards for relief. Resist this urge. It will merely transfer the problem from one pocket to another.

However, if you are sure you can handle credit card debt to deal with a cash emergency, you need to ensure you can pay them off. Otherwise, why add yet another debt?

Think well before borrowing from your 401(k) or Income Retirement Account. There are loopholes that allow this, but also hidden costs, quite apart from potential taxes, penalties and other consequences. Keep in mind that if you were to lose your job, you'd have to repay the loan immediately, or be taxed as though it was a withdrawal. This remedy could be costly in the long run.

Self-Reflection Questions and Actions

1. **Should an emergency arise that requires unexpected expenses, what is your plan?**

2. **Will you borrow from your own savings? Seek a loan from a bank? Other?**

3. **List at least 2 actions you can implement to establish a plan for emergency cash requirements.**

14 AUTOMATED REVENUE STREAMS

We often run into pre-conceived notions people have as objections regarding working in this fashion. You don't have to do any of this if it doesn't fit your style. But, we think it can be helpful rather than being sucked unhappily into the status quo. Many people act shocked when presented with a reasonable modification or adaptation to their working lives.

People often think, "Well, I already work 8 or 10 hours a day and have a family with 2 kids at home to take care after, how am I supposed to do more work on top of that?" That's a valid concern. But, these don't all have to be work on top of more work. It may be up front work to put some systems in place, but many things can be automated now with technology.

Below we will discuss an option using the power of the internet and a few free or low cost tools you could potentially use to set up an automated revenue stream or two.

Earlier, we alluded to the fact that each of us likely has some form of special knowledge, even if you don't know it now, that can be taught to others or is in demand. We live in the information age now. You can design your streams around special or intimate knowledge of particular information you possess and do it for money. An example of a great automated revenue stream is producing and delivering online training (eCourses).

Why eCourses?

Having paid products to offer your customers is a key part of any online business. Traditionally, these have come in the form of eBooks – digital books that can be downloaded and read at leisure.

However, if you're trying to teach something, the eBook isn't always the most popular format. This is where eCourses come in – they are simply digital versions of courses that will deliver information and training in bite-sized, step-by-step chunks.

eCourses are easy to send out because they can be delivered directly via email. And getting into your customer's inbox makes it much more likely that your information will be read!

eCourses have traditionally been seen as an excellent freebie – an incentive to get people to sign up to your mailing list. But eCourses can be products in their own right, and extremely profitable ones at that!

Going Beyond Standard Information Products

When you are trying to think of ways to make more money in your business it's likely that the idea of having a membership website has come up. The volume of money to be made is unlimited, and it comes in month after month. However, the sheer volume of work to do to get that started stops you. And they can be labor intensive.

You'd have to build a secure website with a message board, and a learning center, and then you'd have to monitor it constantly. You don't have that much knowledge of technology so someone quoted you a hefty price tag to build it for you. Money you don't have. The cost of entry into the membership market it just too high.

But, what if I told you that you could make membership volumes of money without having a membership site. Instead, you can create paid eCourses that are delivered automatically to the person who has paid for them. Your only job is to create the eCourse which amounts to writing some articles, loading them into your email list software like Aweber, and setting up a Pay Now button with PayPal? Would you be interested then?

Wordpress + Aweber + PayPal = Dollars

Offering paid eCourses to your audience is truly a lot less hassle than other membership or subscription models. They're an excellent choice if you're limited on time, if you don't want to deal with the techy side of memberships, or if you simply want to work smarter.

All you'll need is two key ingredients: a payment processor and an autoresponder service. It's likely you already have these, but if not, we recommend Aweber and PayPal.

Wordpress. Wordpress is a simple to use website/blog software that has become an industry standard. It lets you easily manage the content over time and there is a giant aftermarket for customizations and additional plugins to add features. We have even produced our own eCourse on how to build a better business blog. It's a 10-part video series. You can download them all for free here: http://goo.gl/WbZRqj

PayPal www.paypal.com : Unless you want to write free eCourses, you're going to need a way for people to send you money to sign up. PayPal is, without a doubt, the top payment processor. Nearly everyone has used it before, and your customers will trust it. You can either create one-time payment buttons, or recurring subscription payments. We'll show you how to do this.

Aweber http://www.aweber.com/?379016: Aweber is an email marketing service that makes it easy for your customers to subscribe to your mailing lists (you can have as many mailing lists and you'd like). You can then set up a sequence of emails to be delivered at an interval you set. You might think you can do this all yourself on your computer, but using an email marketing provider means it's all 100% automated and you won't be limited in the number of recipients you have.

What Will This Cost?

If you're worried about the cost of these two services, don't be! PayPal charges a small fee per transaction, and Aweber starts at just $19 per month (with a 1 month trial for $1). That's far cheaper than setting up complicated membership software, or hiring people to do everything manually!

How Much Money Can You Make?

Think about it: If you built a 12-week course you could charge as little as $20 a week and if you get 10 people to sign up you'll be making $200 a week. That's $200 dollars per week! This is additional revenue that you simply set up and forget about.

If you set up the course right, and market right you're likely to get more than 10 members in any given week. If you write and compile a compelling eCourse it's likely that most of your members will stick with it through the 12 weeks, and there will always be new sign ups because you don't have to start it over. It all runs automatically and you can have any number of people on lesson 1 while some are on lesson 5.

You don't have to have a lot of technical knowledge to start an eCourse membership or subscription. If you currently know how to use your WordPress website, Aweber, and PayPal you can have a membership site set up within a couple of hours. This is what this guide is all about. No fuss, no muss.

Why eCourses = More Money With Less Hassle

If you're not yet convinced about the beauty of the eCourse then here are a few reasons that might help:

No Technical Knowledge Needed

Email eCourses are very easy to set up compared to paid products and memberships. Whether you do a free eCourse or a paid eCourse the steps are pretty much the same. You probably already have a newsletter using email software like Aweber, and you can simply keep using this for your eCourse.

You'll write your eCourse in your favorite text editor, then load up your emails by cutting and pasting them into Aweber. You'll create a PayPal pay button, and the "thank you" page will be the sign up form via Aweber. Your members will sign up, and the delivery of the eCourse is on autopilot!

(Confused? Don't worry – we cover it all step by step later on!)

No Need to Converse With Your Students

When you're running an eCourse, you don't have to ever even talk to your students. Of course, if someone has a problem you may need to deal with some customer service issues - you can let your virtual assistant handle that if something comes up. But since the member is in charge of unsubscribing via PayPal and you'll ensure that this information is available on every single email you send out, there is very likely never going to be any reason to communicate with your students yourself other than within email.

Earn Residual Money for Working Once

An eCourse has the potential to keep earning money years after you have created it. This is called residual income. It's the kind of income where you work once, but keep getting paid well into the future. I created home study courses years ago that other professionals bought online for $400.

How does it work? Well, once you set everything up into your email service (like Aweber) and put a PayPal subscription button on your site, everyone who signs up now and in the future will start at the beginning of the eCourse. As long as you keep your email service and website online, people can sign up for years to come.

You Can Start Making Money Right Away

You don't have to complete your entire eCourse before you start selling it, meaning you can bring that money in fast!

Here's an example – you plan on selling an eCourse that's 12 weeks long before it ends. However, you've only written the first week, so you start selling it right away. You then make sure you write and load each new lesson one week at a time until it's complete. Your customers will never even know it wasn't complete at the time you launched! And, once you're done with all 12 weeks, you're done, for good. Yet, you'll still be bringing in money. It is a good idea to update and improve over time though especially as you receive customer feedback.

You Don't Even Have to Write It

Finally, you don't even have to write the eCourse yourself! An eCourse is the perfect place to compile and use private label rights (PLR). This kind of content is cheaper to buy than unique, ghostwritten content since it's sold to multiple buyers. You can break up any "how to" eBook or report to create a fabulous eCourse that you can make your own and promote.

Just add in some of your own words and make sure the advice is up-to-date, especially if it has to do with technology, and you're done. You can even outsource this entire process to your virtual assistant. Then you can sit back and collect the money.

Are eCourses A Business Model In Themselves?

The great thing about eCourses is that the entire idea can be used as your complete business model. You can simply create a lot of different eCourses for various niches, market them through various sales pages, and make your money just doing that.

Or, you can use eCourses as an addition to your current product funnel. Your eCourse could be one step away from getting customers to sign up to a webinar, teleseminar or other in person event. Or it could be a couple of steps away from one-on-one coaching with you.

In other words, your eCourse can be an end in itself (i.e. profit making business model), or it can be a way to get people used to buying lower-cost products for you before selling higher-ticket programs and services.

eCourses as a Business

If you decide to make eCourses your main business, you can choose more than one niche, create a small website or sales page, Facebook community, Twitter handle, and so on for each niche that you're involved with. Then, using only one Aweber account, you can set up many different eCourse subscriptions.

Once you create each eCourse then you only need to spend time and money marketing the eCourse. If you set up an affiliate program, all the better. The types of eCourses you can set up are truly unlimited. Only your imagination can stop you.

eCourses as Part of Your Product Funnel

It's more likely that paid eCourses (and maybe even free ones) would be an addition to your current product funnel. A free eCourse could be at the widest part of your funnel to get people to sign up for your newsletter. In that case, you can take more liberties with each section of the course and market your other products and services along with the course content.

If you create a paid eCourse, it can be at a smaller point in your product funnel, at a lower price. Afterwards, you might then promote a webinar, or teleseminar and then go on to promote one-on-one coaching. eCourses are a great way to give your audience a taste of your in person offerings.

Earning Residual Income is The Goal

Plus, the very top of your product funnel before one-on-one anything it's always a great idea to seek **residual income**.

Residual income is the only way to make regular money without more work. Residual income means that you worked once and you're making money over and over again without working again (save for smaller maintenance and customer service tasks).

Of course, you will have to continually market your eCourse, but if you set up an affiliate program some of that marketing will also be on autopilot. And if you pay for online traffic or leads, you can set up a budget and let it run automatically as well. If you don't have an affiliate program starting one is not difficult or very technical if you use a good program. Creation of the course is really the easiest part. By far, the hardest part is getting it in front of the right people at the right time. You want to be sure that the information you have is in demand ahead of time and that you make wise choices for targeting high value, but low competition key words. If you do all of that and get enough eyeballs to see it, it should be a success. A little informal market research goes a long way.

Whether you decide to make it your business to create eCourses for a variety of niches or just one, or whether you make an eCourse part of your current product funnel is up to you. And it's perfectly natural for your goals to change over time. Whatever you do, though, you must take action!

eCourse Ideas Worksheet

My eCourse Ideas

Notes: Don't judge any of your ideas! Sometimes you can let yourself think they're not good enough, but just list them all here.

List 10 General eCourse Ideas:

Finding It Hard? Try These Questions:

If you're not finding it easy to come up with good ideas on your own, use these questions to help.

List 5 Problems or Struggles Your Audience Has:

Visit Amazon.com and Find Top Books In Your Niche. Use the "Look Inside" Feature And List Some Chapter Titles Here:

These could later be broken down into step-by-step courses!

eCourse Planning Sheet

Now, take one of the ideas you came up with in step 1. We're going to break it down into a full eCourse.

Main eCourse Topic:

eCourse Delivery Frequency

Every week ☐   2-Weekly ☐   Monthly ☐   Other

How Long Will The eCourse Last? _____
days/ weeks/ months.

How Many Steps Will You Need? _____

For example, a 6 month eCourse, delivered once per week, will need 26 steps.

When Do You Plan to Launch Your eCourse?

Month   /   day   /   Year

Your Outline

Now break up your topic into the number of steps you need. Write each step here. This will form your outline.

eCourse Setup Checklist

Once you've written your eCourse, it's time to set it up. Use this sheet to make sure everything's done.

Welcome Email Written? ☐

First Email of eCourse Written? ☐

PayPal Button Created? ☐

Name of PayPal Button

_____

Aweber List Created? ☐

Name of Aweber List

_____

PayPal Button & Aweber List Linked in Aweber App ☐

Sales Page Created? ☐

Sent Email to Current Customers About New List ☐

Remember to keep writing your eCourse at least one week in advance so that you never fall behind with delivery!

Personal Finance and Investments as Automated Revenue

Getting money out of your business is sometimes tricky. We suggest setting up an automatic billing model in which your clients are charged twice a month either on the first or the 15th of the month. You can tie your own pay in with these payments so that you can more closely replicate a regular pay check. That's one of the hardest things for entrepreneurs to do. The more predictable your revenue, the easier it will be to pay yourself regularly. This is critical if you are to have your business serve your daily, weekly, monthly needs. If you have a simple set up like an LLC, you will take a draw or distribution from the business bank account as your pay. Be sure to put a little away for estimated quarterly taxes or for the end of the tax year. You will be taxed personally in what is called a pass through fashion. Meaning your business is the entity being passed through with regard to imposed taxes onto you personally. Once you have your clients on automatic billing, put yourself on automatic payments too.

Personal Budget. First, in order to make sure that you're profiting at home, you'll need a personal budget so your expenses don't exceed your income which can vary with your own business. This is the equivalent of counting calories for your clients. Budgets are terrible and boring, but they have to be done. Thankfully, more and more technology is making it easier for us. The link at the beginning of this paragraph is to any number of templates you might want to choose from in Google Drive. Choose one that you find simple to use and appropriate for you. Record your monthly transactions as accurately as you can to get an idea of where your money is going. You can also use services like **www.mint.com** which will draw transactions in directly from your online accounts you connect. This is the personal finance version of what www.outirght.com does. Between any business transactions you have and your personal finances, they can be easily managed with these two resources alone.

Checking account. This is where you will conduct most of your personal transactions from. We suggest looking for a local credit union. Although credit unions don't seem to be good with business bank accounts, they are good with personal accounts. This may be a better option than bigger banks as you'll get all the benefits and maybe some better rates and better service. Your share (savings) account will give you a share in the union. The board will also likely be elected. So you'll have more power and more say in your local financial institution in which you choose to do business. You should have a check/debit card that works like a credit card and maybe a check book although more and more people are doing everything digitally these days.

Savings account or rainy day fund. You can keep this account in the same place you'll have your checking account. This is an account you can keep for larger expenses in which you save up for or for unforeseen circumstances or emergencies. This may be a good place to keep your funds you'll need should something happen to your business or you become incapacitated in some way. Financial experts recommend differing total amounts you want to keep in it that range anywhere from three to 12 months. Considering most Americans save very little, even a three month emergency fund can provide a very small safety net for you other people don't have. This is a liquid account you should be able to access quickly and easily and transfer money into and out of almost immediately. You can also fund this account regularly and automatically with a portion of your pay.

Credit account. Once again, you can most likely get a line of credit from the same institution you choose to have checking and savings accounts. A no annual fee, low interest credit card can be good to keep on hand, but only for use in emergencies. Or, use it to build credit or earn rewards or points or miles, but be certain that you can pay it off in full each month or carry a very small balance.

Investment account/money market. A simple and easy way to set this up is through a company [David Bach recommends in his book, The Automatic Millionaire.](#) Sharebuilder. www.sharebuilder.com. You can set up an individual investment account for paper investments. This account also contains with it, a money market account in which you can save money or fund your investments from. A money market account, although not insured, is like a savings account. It still carries risk and the possibility exists that it could lose money, but along with that small risk is the possibility of a slightly higher return than your typical savings account. This is still a liquid account and funds you can get to relatively quickly, but may require 3-5 business days to process transfers to or from other accounts. For investments, you'll want a diversified portfolio across different market sectors. The brokerage you choose may have suggested portfolios based on things like your risk tolerance and age. You can also ask your financial advisor for a specific portfolio. It can be made up of stocks, bonds, mutual funds, exchange traded funds (ETF's), among others.

Retirement account. IRA or 401(k). You will need a retirement account. If you're working for yourself, you will not have an employer to pay you a pension or set up your 401(k) for you. You can speak with one of their customer service reps at Sharebuilder and you may be able to set up a 401(k) for yourself and for any employees you may currently have or have in the future.

You may also choose to set up an Individual Retirement Account or IRA. There are generally two kinds, a traditional and a Roth. You will probably want a Roth IRA. The difference is when the money is taxed. With a traditional IRA account, it is tax deferred. The money is put in non-taxed and then taxed when you withdraw it when you are 65 or older. A Roth IRA is taxed dollars that you can withdraw later without being taxed again after it has compounded. Essentially, it is do you want to be taxed now or later? I personally prefer the Roth IRA because who knows what the tax code will be like decades from now. They could always change it, but I prefer to put it in now under the laws we currently have.

Precious metals. This is a little bit of a wild card. Precious metals can make up around to five or 10% of your invested dollars. It adds another layer of diversification and protection from inflation. Inflation is like a tax in that it makes the value of all the dollars we currently have go down because there is now more paper currency in circulation without being backed up by anything. And that anything is supposed to be gold and silver, but we got off of that system some time ago. Now, you can invest in gold and silver and other metals to act as a hedge against inflationary time period or, god forbid, a major economic disaster. At present time of writing this, a simple silver one dollar coin is actually worth about $21 dollars simply because of the value of the metal from which it is made. An equal amount of gold is over $1300

Generally speaking, when the stock market does well, precious metals go down. When the stock market is doing poorly, or inflation is high, gold and silver do very well. Precious metals also tend to do well when there is uncertainty in other areas of the economy or geopolitical turmoil in the world like in oil producing nations. Again, precious metals act mostly like a hedge or protection against these things. Keep in mind, that all of these things have their value rooted in faith. National currencies have lost their values relatively quickly. Gold has demonstrated an element of staying power over millennia. These metals can have intrinsic industrial value, but as currency, the value is still driven by faith which could, in theory, fall in and out of favor at any time.

Self-Reflection Questions and Actions

1. **Using this chapter as a resource, list those tools (such as PayPal, Aweber, etc.) that you envision using.**

2. **Will you offer your clients/partners eCourses? Will you produce a blog using WordPress or another service provider?**

3. **List at least 2 actions you can implement to move forward.**

15 ADDITIONAL RESOURCES

There are many, probably infinite, ways of living your life in a prosperous fashion. Ideally, our tips will match your personality, characteristics, and nature and help you take ownership and pride in whatever you choose to do. Use the information, examples and tools in the appendix as a springboard to new ventures.

The following will apply directly to American employees, but may not be as relevant to readers outside the United States.

You might be thinking, "but I need medical benefits." If I start on this venture, I won't be full-time and won't get the benefits I would with a full-time job in a larger company.

Here's a little secret. Do you know why companies first started paying for your health insurance? It was so they could get away with paying you less cash! Seriously! Health care costs have risen so much, however, that it has backfired. Worse, we now *demand* employers make these offers. It might be better to take that cash equivalent of your health costs and get your own care.

While the sentiment that you'll go without some benefits might be partially true in terms of company stock, it's not true in terms of other benefits from an average employer. We're not saying you can't have a full-time position as your primary source of income with all the benefits that go with it. Just don't rely on that solely.

This is a new type of economy, a new job economy. If you leave it to your full-time employer to give you the benefits you want, you're not managing the power well. Such benevolence belongs to them. Benefits exist only as long as you work there.

If you are self-employed or choose to put together a career in a multiple stream fashion, you can, nonetheless, find access to the same or better benefits that a larger company would provide.

Socialized health care costs might mean you can come out ahead. You won't be on the hook to pay for the risks of others. And it might even be a tax haven if you can get a plan that's more appropriate for you. It might be possible to take the cash equivalent of what a company would pay you in benefits, shop around for a cheaper option and make a profit (in real dollars).

That, of course, depends on the company and your area. And here's the best thing: if you leave your company or lose your job, the company owns your account having paid for it. You're part of its "group." Find a new job that offers something similar.

With our method and the resources we provide below, these accounts can belong to you, the person, not you, your position (job). Wherever you go and whatever you do, it is your account. For example, HSA stands for health savings account. It is actually a tax haven for you, not a tax burden for others. It works essentially like an IRA for your health costs.

Currently you can deposit up to $5,000 per year for use on health costs. It must be connected with a high deductible plan. But, the good thing about high deductible plans is that they have low premiums. So if you are young, healthy, and single, you have really low costs; about $72 per month in premiums. If you happen to reach a deductible of, say, $1,500, then regular insurance will kick in. Some companies, like Whole Foods Market, give one of these accounts to each of their employees and contribute to it as well.

Couple this with a doctor in your community who is fee-for-service and does not take insurance. Much of what is provided is routine and can be done over the phone or by email. If a consultation is necessary, we have a prepaid plan for the year based on time, not the procedure. No co-pays or any of that confusing mess is needed as 80 per cent of what is done in an ER, can be done in an office, which also keeps costs down. If you need to see a doctor, you can get same-day appointments. If you have regular insurance, you can get reimbursed. Better yet doctors still make house calls, especially for older patients. It's a great way to get the care that is needed while skirting the whole political mess involving traditional insurance plans. Look in your area for fee-for-service doctors. All you are doing is paying a doctor for his time – the same way you would pay the plumber, electrician, mechanic, or any other service provider.

It's helpful with resources like this to ask yourself if there are other ways of doing things. Can you meet your needs through other means or avenues? Maybe there is a smarter way of doing things than the status quo. It's worth exploring. Because something like healthcare is such a hot, emotionally charged, political issue, most people refuse to believe it can be anything other than one way. That's not true. That's not true with hardly anything in the world.

One of my favorite resources is The Garrett Planning Network, www.garrettplanningnetwork.com. It's a nationwide network of independent, fee-only financial advisors. Whether you are a do-it-yourselfer seeking a professional opinion, looking for periodic financial guidance, or merely ongoing assistance objective financial advice can be obtained. The network can answer these types of questions:

Am I on track to achieve my financial goals?

What can I do better, smarter or cheaper to meet my goals?

How much exposure to the stock market should I have?
When should I start social security?

How much life insurance do I need?

Join a mastermind group: This is a group of professionals of like mind who are trying to grow their businesses and hold each other accountable to action items to do so. The concept first came about from Napoleon Hill in his book, *Think and Grow Rich*.

Use vendors: Don't be afraid to partner up with other vendors to provide services that you can't or don't want to do. Don't forget about Fiverr. Maintain the relationship and continue to work with them.

Brokering services and subcontracting work is another option. Just like brokered removal services with your own vehicle, you can do the same with your businesses. Essentially, you'll be operating as the middleman. Although margins might be cut, it could save you time and effort. Get a contractor to perform the work. Use the additional time to drum up more customers, even if with smaller margins.

Join associations in your field that offer the support and tools to perform your skill or service more effectively and efficiently. They may offer discounts on important items, such as liability insurance.

Join networking groups. Check with your local chamber of commerce or other organizations such as Business Networking International, www.bni.com for networking groups in your area. It is crucial that you move out of your comfort zone to meet new people and drum up new prospects. Once you get the hang of it, these activities are actually quite fun. Other organizations also specialize in professional networking.

Attend as many events as possible. You'll have to make a cost choice as going to a lot of them can add up. One or two new clients a year from chamber activities, is worthwhile but obviously aim for more Large breakfasts and after hours mixers events can also be fun and fairly productive.

Our networking group is the most productive for us. It's a smaller, but closer group where members join to share leads. You get exclusivity in the group. We meet twice a month for lunch or breakfast. Each member gets 30 seconds to introduce themselves and give an elevator speech. You'll want to have a standard, scripted elevator speech and not just wing it. You'll sound a lot more professional and deliver vital information.

Your most successful conversions to clients will be qualified leads. In other words, if you run across someone who needs to sell a house, try to get permission for the realtor in the group to give them a call or email to discuss the options using his/her services. It is rare to convert referrals from someone who merely gives a name and number, as calls are rarely returned. Try to get the person providing the service or product to get in touch with the prospect. If you can do this, you'll be far ahead of the rest of the group.

Luncheons and expos are always potentially useful. These may be more appropriate for a schedule that involves a lot of after normal work hours. However, it is vital that you make time to get out and continuously network so that you drive prospective clients into your marketing funnel.

Making the Most of Your One-on-One Networking Meetings with Other Professionals

When you're out networking you'll likely be in a group or attending an event with many people. It's possible to develop relationships and get more leads this way, but think of it as a process – especially if you are a member of a networking group.

You'll need to take it a step further to meet other members and professionals in the area in a one-on-one meeting. This allows you to get to know them and their business better, and vice versa. A lunch somewhere neutral but ideally at your facility, if you have one, is a start. You can offer to bring lunch for them so they can see your place and where you operate.

To maximize the potential value of such a meeting, which can easily deteriorate into shop talk, there are a few preliminary steps. Keeping on track is important, especially if you want to sound organized and professional.

A day or two before the meeting, send an email with a description of your target market and what kinds of leads you are seeking. Keep it simple and clear. Be a giver! The more you give, the more you get. Here's an example for a personal trainer:

"Dear Mrs. Smith,
I will see you tomorrow at Panera Leesburg at 12 pm. If you have a few minutes when you get home, reply to this email with a description of who you are looking for as referral leads and I'll try to bring a couple of names to the meeting.

We are looking for more one-on-one training clients or small groups of two or three people for reduced rate training. Our target market is a middle-aged person, most likely a women, married, with dual income who lives in or close to Ashburn. We also target business owners, busy professionals, and entrepreneurs as they are very busy and can benefit from our program. They would generally like to lose body fat, improve strength, shape, stamina, and achieve certain health markers in a safe and time-efficient program (30 minutes). We've had success with managing diabetes, osteoporosis, and arthritis.

If there's anything else I could help bring to the table please let me know.

Thank you."

At the meeting, stand and greet the person with a firm handshake. Review this simple outline to keep on track, maximize your time, and get the most out of your meeting.

1. Information about your businesses: Take turns offering some background and history about yourself and your business. Focus on current products or services. Keep it simple and offer your core service. Don't confuse them. You want them to remember you as the one who offers a particular service in your local area.

2. Target market: Let the other person know exactly what kind of lead or referral you are looking for and/or a description of your target market. The more descriptive the better for them. Also, let them know the best way for a lead or referral to contact you. Inform your colleague of your unique selling proposition. What makes you or your business better, cheaper, or different to that of your competitors?

3. Possible leads: Ideally, if you have a name or two with you, get the person you are meeting call the person who is the lead. You'll need to get their (the lead's) permission to have your colleague give them a call or email. This is the best probability of turning it into a closed transaction. Try to have them do the same for you. We *rarely* convert leads when someone merely told them to call. Those people almost never call. You need to be proactive, get contact information for the lead you are given so that you can call yourself.

Follow up: If you can't bring leads to the meeting, don't stop there. Make a plan to reconnect with a phone call or email three to five days after you've had some time to digest your colleague's information and have looked through you contacts to see how you can find a match.

Follow this outline and you'll stay on track. It should only take an hour. You'll greatly increase both of your chances of obtaining more leads from your efforts. Hopefully, it will evolve into a long and lucrative relationship with fellow professionals in your area.

Self-Reflection Questions and Actions

1. **Using this chapter as a resource, list any other additional resources you will need for your multiple streams.**

2. **How can you most effectively meet and network with other professionals?**

3. **List at least 2 actions you can take to move forward.**

APPENDIX

Develop Your Network and Prospects for New Business

Next to each job or industry listed below, write down the names and numbers or email of anyone you know, however remotely, in this industry. This is to establish your network and sphere of influence with people you currently know or with whom you have an association. Work backwards from an annual revenue goal with the prospecting goal setting worksheet.

Next, use the scripts below to call or email people (not cold calling, but business associates you already know) in your network who might know a good candidate for what you do. Follow-up scripts and lead qualification questions are also included.

Finally, use the daily call reporting worksheet below to keep track of your efforts.

We do this all the time, especially through email or other social media such as Facebook and LinkedIn with awesome results. Add this to your arsenal and teach it to your trainers and they may have some good results over time.

A	J
Actor	Jeweler
Actuary	Jockey
Advertising	Joiner and Wood machinist
Advocate	Journalist
Aeronautical Engineer	
Aerospace Industry Trades	K
Agricultural Economist	Knitter
Agricultural Engineer	
Agricultural Extension Officer	L
Agricultural Inspector	Laborer
Agricultural Technician	Land Surveyor
Agriculture	Landscape Architect
Agriculturist	Law
Agronomist	Learner Official
Air Traffic Controller	Leather Chemist
Ambulance Emergency Care Worker	Leather Worker

Animal Scientist
Anthropologist
Aquatic Scientist
Archaeologist
Architect
Architectural Technologist
Archivist
Area Manager

Armament Fitter
Armature Winder
Art Editor
Artist
Assayer Sampler
Assembly Line Worker
Assistant Draughtsman
Astronomer
Attorney
Auctioneer
Auditor
Automotive Body Repairer
Automotive Electrician
Automotive Mechanic
Automotive Trimmer

B
Babysitting Career
Banking Career
Beer Brewing
Biochemist
Biokineticist
Biologist
Biomedical Engineer
Biomedical Technologist
Blacksmith
Boilermaker
Bookbinder
Bookkeeper
Botanist
Branch Manager
Bricklayer
Bus Driver
Business Analyst
Business Economist
Butler

C
Cabin Attendant
Carpenter
Cartographer
Cashier
Ceramics Technologist
Chartered Accountant
Chartered Management Accountant
Chartered Secretary
Chemical Engineer

Lecturer
Librarian
Life-guard
Lift Mechanic
Light Delivery Van Driver
Linesman
Locksmith

M
Machine Operator
Machine Worker
Magistrate
Mail Handler
Make-up Artist
Management Consultant
Manager
Marine Biologist
Marketing
Marketing Manager
Materials Engineer
Mathematician
Matron
Meat Cutting Technician
Mechanical Engineer
Medical Doctor
Medical Orthotist Prosthetist
Medical Physicist
Merchandise Planner
Messenger
Meteorological Technician
Meteorologist
Meter-reader
Microbiologist
Miner
Mine Surveyor
Mining Engineer
Model Builder
Model
Motor Mechanic
Musician

N
Nature Conservator
Navigating Officer
Navigator
Nuclear Scientist
Nursing
Nutritionist

O
Occupational Therapist
Oceanographer
Operations Researcher
Optical Dispenser
Optical Technician
Optometrist

Chemist	Ornithologist
Chiropractor	
City Treasurer	P
Civil Engineer	Painter and Decorator
Civil Investigator	Paint Technician
Cleaner	Paper Technologist
Clergyman	Patent Attorney
Clerk	Personal Trainer
Clinical Engineering	Personnel Consultant
Clinical Technologist	Petroleum Technologist
Clothing Designer	Pharmacist Assistant
Clothing Manager	Pharmacist
Coal Technologist	Photographer
Cobbler	Physicist
Committee Clerk	Physiologist
Computer Industry	Physiotherapist
Concrete Technician	Piano Tuner
Conservation and Wildlife	Pilot
Construction Manager	Plumber
Copy Writer	Podiatrist
Correctional Services	Police Officer
Costume Designer	Post Office Clerk
Crane Operator	Power Plant Operator
Credit Controller	Private Secretary
Crop Protection and Animal Health	Production Manager
Customer and Excise Officer	Projectionist
Customer Service Agent	Project Manager
	Psychologist
D	Psychometrist
Dancer	Public Relations Practitioner
Database Administrator	Purchasing Manager
Data Capturer	
Dealer in Oriental Carpets	Q
Decor Designer	Quality Control Inspector
Dental Assistant and Oral Hygienist	Quantity Surveyor
Dental Technician	
Dental Therapist	R
Dentist	Radiation Protectionist
Detective	Radio
Diamond Cutting	Radiographer
Diesel Fitter	Receptionist
Diesel loco Driver	Recreation Manager
Diesel Mechanic	Rigger
Die-sinker and Engraver	Road Construction Plant Operator
Dietician	Roofer
Diver	Rubber Technologist
DJ	
Domestic Appliance Mechanic	S
Domestic Personnel	Salesperson
Domestic radio and Television Mechanic	Sales Representative
Domestic Worker	Saw Operator
Draughtsman	Scale Fitter
Driver and Stacker	Sea Transport Worker
	Secretary
E	Security Officer
Earth Moving Equipment Mechanic	Sheetmetal Worker

Ecologist	Shop Assistant
Economist Technician	Shopfitter
Editor	Singer
Eeg Technician	Social Worker
Electrical and Electronic Engineer	Sociologist
Electrical Engineering Technician	Soil Scientist
Electrician	Speech and Language Therapist
Electrician (Construction)	Sport Manager
Engineering	Spray Painter
Engineering Technician	Statistician
Entomologist	Swimming Pool Superintendent
Environmental Health Officer	Systems Analyst
Estate Agent	
Explosive Expert	T
Explosive Technologist	Tailor
Extractive Metallurgist	Taxidermist
	Teacher
F	Technical Illustrator
Farmer	Technical Writer
Farm Foreman	Teller
Farm Worker	Terminologist
Fashion Buyer	Textile Designer
Film and Production	Theatre Technology
Financial and Investment Manager	Tourism Manager
Fire-Fighter	Traffic Officer
Fireman at the Airport	Translator
Fitter and Turner	Travel Agent
Flight Engineer	Typist
Florist	
Food Scientist and Technologist	V
Footwear	Valuer and Appraiser
Forester Service	Vehicle Driver
Funeral Director	Veterinary Nurse
Furrier	Veterinary Surgeon
	Viticulturist
G	
Game Ranger	W
Gardener	Watchmaker
Geneticist	Weather Observer
Geographer	Weaver
Geologist	Welder
Geotechnologist	Wood Scientist
Goldsmith and Jeweler	Wood Technologist
Grain Grader	
Graphic Designer	Y
Gravure machine Minder	Yard Official
H	Z
Hairdresser	Zoologist
Herpetologist	
Home Economist	
Homoeopath	
Horticulturist	
Hospitality Industry	
Hospital Porter	
Human Resource Manager	

Hydrologist I Ichthyologist Industrial Designer Industrial Engineer Industrial Engineering Technologist Industrial Technician Inspector Instrument Maker Insurance Interior Designer Interpreter Inventory and Store Manager	

Prospecting Goal Setting

Work backwards from your annual income goal. Statistically, over a 12-month period, you should be on track to reach your goal.

Annual Income Goal: _____

Personal Income Per Deal: _____

Number of Deals Needed: _____

Monthly Deals Needed: _____

Consultations Needed/Deal: _____

Consultations Needed/Month: _____

Leads Needed/Consultation: _____

Leads Needed/Month: _____

Contacts Needed/Leads: _____

Contacts Needed/Month: _____

Days Worked/Month: _____

Contacts Needed/ Day: _____

Prospecting Script for Center of Influence

(Call people you know from your Market Development Inventory)

Hi, this is _____. This is a business call. Is this a good time to talk for a minute? Who do you know that could benefit from the type of training services we offer? Can you think of anyone in your (church group, family, neighborhood, or office) who may need my services at this time? Great! Would you mind if I gave them a call or email? By the way, do you currently work with a trainer or go to a gym? Terrific!

Client Just Signed Script (a day or two after sign-up)

Hi Mrs. Jones, this is_____ from S.P.A.R.T.A. Thank you again for coming in and signing up with us. I'm really excited about how you're going to do. While I think of it, most of the business we do is word of mouth. Do you know of anyone who would like to be part of or could benefit from our program as you're about to? Great! Would you mind if I gave them a call or email? Thank you very much!

Script for calling the prospect

Hi Mrs. Smith, my name is_____ from S.P.A.R.T.A. This is a sales call about our new program. Is this a good time? Your friend, Mrs. Jones, just signed up to join our exercise program with goals of improving her body shape and increasing strength and stamina and mentioned your name as someone that might be interested in and could benefit from a program like this. Did you know we offer FREE consultations which includes a FREE workout with a certified trainer? Would you like to set one up? Which time is better for you, Monday at XXX pm or Tuesday at XXX pm? Great! Thanks for taking the time to speak with me. I'll see you Monday at XXX pm.

Pre-Qualification Questions

Pre-Qualify 100% of prospects. You can mix these questions in smoothly upon the prospect's first call to you.

- How did you hear about me/us?
- What are you trying to achieve from working out?
- Are you planning to interview more than one trainer?
- Are you working out on your own currently?
- Can you fit two or three workouts per week in your schedule?
- Is this 100 per cent your decision or do you have to discuss this with somebody?
- If you feel this program is right for you, can you afford ($?$?$?) per session/month? Or …
- My clients currently pay $60 per session. Does that work for you?
- If, after the workout you feel this is right for you, are you ready to start right away?

And, of course, keep track of your prospecting efforts to make sure you are staying on track for your annual goal.

Daily Call Reporting

Summary of Daily Total Numbers (from above):

Monday:					Thursday:

Contacts:_____			Contacts:_____

Consults:_____			Consults:_____

Contracts:_____			Contracts:_____

Tuesday:				Friday:

Contacts: _____			Contacts:_____

Consults:_____			Consults:_____

Contracts:_____			Contracts:_____

Wednesday:				Weekly Totals:

Contacts:_____			Contacts:_____

Consults:_____			Consults:_____

Contracts:_____			Contracts:_____

Business Plan

The business plan should prove that the business will generate enough revenue to cover expenses and make a satisfactory return for bankers or investors should you need any. There are a number of ways of formulating a business plan but each should contain certain essential sections.

The Basics

Provide an executive summary of less than two pages at the start of the business plan. This sells the plan and highlights its features. A company summary should be included containing a factual description of the company, its owners and history. A section referring to products and or services and their points of difference in the market should go next.

It is also essential to include a market analysis. This provides a summary of typical customers, a list of competitors, and refers to market size and expected growth. Another important section would set out strategies and implementation that describe how the product and plan would be sold and put into action, together with predicted milestones. A financial plan indicating sales, cash flow and profits and a description of the management team, its collective experience and key accomplishments should be spelled out in a management summary.

Individuals can either hire a professional to write a business plan or attempt their own making use of excellent business planning software or books that are available.

Once funding has been raised and a business is operating the business plan serves as a road map. It is not a static document. It needs to be referred to in order to ensure that the business remains focused, on track and meets its milestones.

A market evaluation is a useful analysis of a company's success. It is a big but invaluable undertaking. It involves a range of areas including sales figures that refer to specific time frames and events, marketing goals, advertising content and the media mix being utilized to determine whether expectations have been met, failed or exceeded.

Also necessary is a marketing goals analysis. Is the business taking that market? Is it the most profitable market for the company? An analysis must show an increase, or otherwise, in the market share and by how much.

Have advertisements fulfilled their purpose? Did the target market understand and respond to the message in the advertisements? By evaluating the use and efficiency of the media mix and checking on the creation process, the cost effectiveness of the particular program can be checked along with which sections of media attracted the most market share.

A separate section should include ideas for future improvement.

Analyze Competition

This can be the most difficult section in a business plan. The first step of the competitive analysis is to determine the local competition. This can be done quite simply by observing, through internet searches and a telephone directory.

The main question will be one of range and finding out how far customers are prepared to travel to obtain your competitor's goods and services. Some businesses also have non-local competitors such as mail order companies or online stores.

What market or market segments do they serve and what benefits do they offer? Why do customers buy from them, what do they buy, how much do they charge and what promotions are visible?

Checking websites and visiting a business should provide information about the products and customer treatment by the competition.

A company's vendors, suppliers and employees are good sources of information as are trade fairs where competitors exhibit. Once the information has been gathered it needs to be analyzed, particularly to determine a niche market that can be targeted with alternative offers.

The goal of the analysis is to identify and expand your competitive advantage by focusing on the benefits your business can offer that the competitor can't or won't.

Statistics are stacked against new businesses succeeding. "Businesses with fewer than 20 employees have only a 37 per cent chance of surviving four years and just a nine per cent chance of surviving 10 years ... Restaurants fare worse with a 20 per cent chance of surviving just two years. Of these failed businesses only 10 per cent closed involuntary due to bankruptcy. The remaining 90 per cent closed because the business was not successful, did not provide the level of income desired, or was too much work" according to research by the US Small Business Administration.

We've heard that "people don't plan to fail they fail to plan". That's particularly true of business. All businesses should have a clear plan for success and an alternative if things go wrong.

There are three factors linked to success. They are a business plan; detailed financial information about the intended business and an accurate profile of the target market.

Use this template below to help you craft a full business plan or to get direction for the start of your venture. Even if you're not starting a whole new business, you can use this worksheet for each new project taken on as a revenue stream. Consider each new project a "business" within itself.

Business Plan Worksheet

What is your business model(s)? **Description of business (Executive Summary consider writing last):** **Vision?** **Mission?**
Who is your target market(s)? (summary from Marketing Plan)
Your Unique Selling Proposition • What are you offering?   • What problem does it solve?

- What is different about you?

- What are your revenue channels?

- Who is your competition?

- Why should people buy from you vs. the competition?

Business Goals
(summary from goal setting worksheet)

- Long Term Goals

- Short Term Goals

- Who is your management team?

SWOT Analysis

- What are you top strengths?

- What are your top weaknesses?

- What are your key opportunities for success?

- What are the threats to your business?

Business Growth and Exit Strategies

- What is your growth strategy?

- What is your exit strategy?

Business Profitability:
(combine all projects plus general business expenses and other revenue)

Total Estimated Expenses (total expenses for all projects combined and general business expenses)	
Total Estimated Revenue (total revenue for all projects combined)	
Total Estimated Profit (total revenue – total profit)	
Estimated Return on Investment (total profit/total expense)	
Estimated Growth Annual	
Estimated 3-5 Year Growth	

Note: If not including your time in expenses, estimate the value of your time per project by calculating:

Total Profit for Project:
Total Hours Spent:
Hourly Profit:

Marketing Plan

(complete one for each project, if you have more than one)

Project 1:

Target Market Description: (size, demographics, buying characteristics, problems, etc)	
Marketing Strategy 1:	**Key tasks:** • • • •
Marketing Strategy 2:	**Key tasks:**

	•
	•
Marketing Strategy 3:	**Key tasks:** • •
Marketing Strategy 4:	**Key tasks:** • •
Marketing Strategy 5:	**Key tasks:** • •
Marketing Strategy 6:	**Key tasks:** • •
Marketing Strategy 7:	**Key tasks:** • •

Action Plan

Initial Project Set Up Tasks	Deadline	Responsibility

Ongoing Tasks – Per Project	Deadline	Responsibility

Ongoing Business Tasks (overall business)	Deadline	Responsibility

Potential Obstacles

Obstacle	Resource/Solution	Where to Find It

Other Notes:

Profitability Analysis

(do estimates on separate spreadsheet, per month and year)

Project Profitability:

(complete for each project)

Total Estimated Expenses (total expenses for individual project)	
Total Estimated Revenue (total revenue for individual project)	
Total Estimated Profit	

(total revenue – total profit)	
Estimated Return on Investment **(total profit/total expense)**	

(For your convenience, 16 sample ideas have been added)

Ways to find leads in your market.

1. Create a referral program to provide incentive for your current clients to refer you more. FREE.

2. Put simple free daily ads on www.craigslist.org, www.backpage.com, and similar sites. Use more than one category. Advertise a FREE consultation or a FREE eBook for responders. Continue to follow up with your inquiries. FREE.

3. Place business cards and brochures in grocery stores or coffee houses with community bulletin boards. Use www.vistaprint.com to produce them. FREE or very low cost.

4. Write a FREE eBook or report. Put it on your website for download in exchange for email addresses. FREE.

5. Launch a website. $20 per year.

6. Start a blog. Go to Wordpress, www.wordpress.com and set one up. Put up content-rich information at least once a week for your niche. FREE.

7. Collect emails for your email prospect list so you can directly communicate and market to prospective clients. Send out a

content-rich newsletter twice a month. FREE. Use the Outlook distribution list if you have 30 clients or under. Or graduate to a better newsletter service as you grow such as www.aweber.com which costs about $19 a month.

8. Call former clients and try to tempt them with a special offer once a month. FREE.

9. Provide gift cards to your clients for their friends for a FREE consultation and FREE workout. FREE.

10. Allocate gift cards to your network of business associates to hand out to THEIR clients as gifts. FREE.

11. Go to chamber of commerce events and network. Meet new people every day. Join a business networking group. Go into it trying to pass leads and referrals first, then they will refer to you. Costs about $250 to 300 per year.

12. When starting out, get a few friends or loose acquaintances to use your service and give you testimonials. Mostly FREE.

13. Place a box in similar businesses with a great offer for people who deposit their business card inside. Leave it at hair salons, tanning salons, bridal shops, spas, places people frequent where they are likely to talk about your service. Offer something in return to the owners like referring your clients to them. FREE.

14. Prospect daily! Use your scripts and call your contacts to dig up leads for people they know who may benefit from your service. This may take 10 to 30 calls and or emails a day for new leads. FREE. Prospecting scripts are provided earlier in the book.

15. Ask current clients what they would like or what they think is missing or could be performed better that might provide another revenue stream. FREE.

16. Speak in public. Give a seminar or workshop. Look for joint venture partners to put on events or raise money for charitable causes. FREE.

Sample Contractor/Consultant Agreement

Company Logo   Company Name
Address
Email address

CONSULTANT/SUBCONTRACTOR AGREEMENT

This Consultant/Subcontractor Agreement ("this Agreement") is made and entered into as of _____ by and between COMPANY X, LLC ("COMPANY X"), a Virginia limited liability company, _____ having an address at _____ and a _____ corporation (if applicable) having a place of business at _____ ("Consultant"). COMPANY X and Consultant desire to enter into an agreement whereby Consultant will provide certain services to, and perform certain work for, COMPANY X. The parties hereto agree as follows:

DEFINITIONS:
"Consultant" means the individual specified above.

"Firm, Fixed Price" or "FFP" shall mean one price to provide certain specified and described Services.

"Hourly Fee" or "T&M" shall mean a fixed rate per hour paid for all Services provided, with additional expenses or materials paid for at "cost" or at "cost plus a handling charge."

"Services" means, as the context requires, the services to be performed by Consultant hereunder.

"Task Order(s)" means that document issued with reference to this Agreement which describes the Services to be provided by the Consultant when and as ordered by COMPANY X.

"Work Product" means, as the context requires, any software, ideas, concepts, techniques, inventions, processes, writings or works of authorship developed, created and/or provided by Consultant during the course of performing the Services and embodied, in whole or in part, in Consultant's deliverable(s) to COMPANY X or to a COMPANY X client.

COMPENSATION AND PAYMENT:
(a) COMPANY X agrees to pay Consultant for performance of Services in accordance with the Task Orders issued under this Agreement. A labor rate, applicable to all Task Orders unless otherwise stated in the Task Order, is specified in Exhibit B, attached hereto. If an hourly rate is specified, Consultant's time shall be computed to the nearest one quarter of an hour; and, if a daily rate is specified, a day shall consist of not less than eight hours of work. If an estimated cost for a Time and Material or Labor Hour rate agreement is specified on a Task Order, Consultant shall not exceed the estimated cost without prior written approval of COMPANY X. Further, COMPANY X will not pay Consultant in excess of the estimated cost of a Task Order without prior written approval.

(b) Consultant shall invoice COMPANY X based on work actually performed under a Task Order either (i) within seven working days after the end of each calendar month during which work was performed; or (ii) when compensation is due and payable in accordance with a specific Task Order. Such invoice shall specify the Task Order number, address to which payment shall be submitted, the hourly or daily rate and the hours or days actually worked if a Task Order is performed on a Time and Materials basis, and other relevant information.

(c) Provided Consultant's invoice and supporting documentation are acceptable, payment of Consultant's invoice will be made by COMPANY X within fifteen (15) days of COMPANY X's receipt of payment by its client(s), if Consultant's work was performed specifically for one COMPANY X client. Otherwise, COMPANY X will pay within thirty (30) days of invoice receipt. The Consultant will submit its invoices to COMPANY X via email to: email address or by regular mail to:

COMPANY X, LLC
Address

(d) If authorized in advance of expenditure, Consultant will be reimbursed for all reasonable and necessary expenses incurred in the course of business for travel outside of the greater metropolitan area of Consultant's principle place of business. Greater metropolitan area shall mean at a radius of more than 50 miles from Consultant's place of business. Consultant is not entitled to any advances for travel expenses. Consultant shall not be reimbursed for any mileage, parking fees, meals and similar expenses for travel within a 50 mile radius of Consultant's principle place of business, unless such reimbursement has been specified in a Task Order.
(1) Consultant shall obtain air travel at the least expensive rate available consistent with meeting the travel requirements of providing the Services in a reasonable timeframe. Unless otherwise authorized, meal, hotel and private automobile expenses shall not exceed the amounts specified on Exhibit B.
(2) Consultant shall complete an expense report form, and provide supporting receipts for all expenditures except for meals under $25.00. Such expense reports shall be submitted to COMPANY X within three business days of the conclusion of such travel.

(e) Nothing herein shall be deemed to constitute a waiver of COMPANY X's right to dispute and refuse to pay, in whole or in part, claims for compensation or reimbursable expenses if Consultant has materially misrepresented his or her capacity to perform an accepted assignment, failed to substantially accomplish satisfactorily the results specified, or otherwise materially breached any provision of this Agreement.

TERM:
This Agreement will become effective on the date first set forth above and shall continue in twelve (12) month increments unless written notice is provided by either party sixty (60) days prior to the end of the then-current twelve (12) month period, or until terminated in accordance with the "Termination" clause. The term of each Task Order will be stated in the Task Order and such term shall run independently of the term of this Agreement.

SERVICES:
Consultant agrees to provide the type of Services set forth in Exhibit A as and when specifically ordered under Task Orders referencing this Agreement. COMPANY X may, at any time, increase or decrease the scope of the Services and/or Work Product specifically ordered under a Task Order, provided that any change requiring additional services shall be subject to the parties' mutual agreement regarding Consultant's compensation in connection therewith. Any such agreement regarding additional compensation shall be set forth in a signed, written amendment to the relevant Task Order.

TASK ORDERS:
As stated under the clause entitled "Services," all work under this Agreement shall be ordered by Task Orders. A sample Task Order form may be found in Exhibit C. Each Task Order shall be bilaterally executed and shall state, at a minimum, the following information:

(a) the type of contractual arrangement for the individual Task Order—e.g., Firm, Fixed Price (FFP), Time and Materials (T&M) etc.;
(b) the Statement of Work for the Task Order;
(c) the Period of Performance for the Task Order;
(d) the price(s) for the work to be performed;
(e) the payment schedule, if applicable, for the work to be performed;
(f) that the Task Order is issued under the terms of this Agreement; and
(g) any special terms and conditions for the Task Order, including the incorporation of COMPANY X's client terms and conditions, if applicable.

Each Task Order shall be treated as a part of this Agreement but shall be severable and segregable from this Agreement with respect to the term of the Task Order, the price or estimated cost, the payment amount, the Statement of Work (SOW), any additional Special Terms and Conditions and any other similar terms which would clearly be applicable only to the specific Task Order in which those terms appear. If this Agreement is terminated in accordance with the "Termination" clause or the "Term" clause, this Agreement shall not be considered terminated in its entirety until the end of the period of performance of each and every Task Order which was not specifically terminated by the termination notice.

METHOD OF PERFORMANCE AND SUPERVISION:
Consultant will generally determine the method, details and means of performing the Services. COMPANY X shall not have the right to control the exact manner or determine the precise method of accomplishing the Services; however, COMPANY X shall be entitled to exercise a broad, general right of supervision and control over the results of the Services performed to ensure satisfactory performance. This power of supervision shall include the right to inspect, stop work, make suggestions or recommendations as to the details of the work, and request modifications to the scope of the Services.

SCHEDULING AND REPORTING:
Requirements for written reports, if any, shall be specified in the individual Task Orders.

PLACE OF WORK:
Consultant will perform the Services at Consultant's own office or work site unless otherwise designated on the individual Task Order.

RIGHT TO REJECT:
COMPANY X reserves the right, in its sole reasonable discretion, to reject the Services, and Consultant agrees that he/she shall immediately cease any work under this Agreement if such a rejection occurs. Reasons for rejection may include, but are not limited to, poor performance, threatening behavior, intoxication, drug use and similar behaviors which might impair the timely and professional provision of Services under this Agreement.

NON-EXCLUSIVE RELATIONSHIP:
This Agreement is non-exclusive. Consultant shall retain the right to perform work for other parties during the term of this Agreement, and COMPANY X may have work of the same or a similar kind performed by its own personnel or other contractors or consultants during the term of this Agreement.

CONFLICT OF INTEREST:
Consultant will report to COMPANY X during the term of this Agreement about any and all contracts, agreements, understandings, prior employment or prior relationships applicable to Consultant, which may prohibit, restrict or limit Consultant's performance of this Agreement.

INDEPENDENT CONTRACTOR STATUS:
The parties hereto acknowledge and agree that Consultant is an independent contractor to

COMPANY X and not an employee, agent, joint venturer or partner of COMPANY X. Consultant further acknowledges and agrees that, as an independent contractor, Consultant will not be entitled to (1) make a claim for unemployment, worker's compensation or disability pursuant to this Agreement or Consultant's relationship with COMPANY X, or (2) receive any vacation, health, retirement or other benefits pursuant to this Agreement or Consultant's relationship with COMPANY X. COMPANY X will not (a) withhold FICA from its payments to Consultant, (b) make state or federal unemployment insurance contributions on behalf of Consultant, or (c) withhold state and federal income taxes from its payments to Consultant. Consultant hereby represents and warrants to COMPANY X that, except as otherwise expressly provided herein, all activities and work performed by Consultant under this Agreement shall be at Consultant's own risk and liability. Consultant's taxpayer identification number and local business license/permit number, if applicable, are set forth on Exhibit B.

INTELLECTUAL PROPERTY:
(a) COMPANY X owns all rights, title and interest in all Work Products provided by Consultant under this Agreement, including but not limited to all copyrights, trade secrets and other forms of intellectual property rights, and all Work Products shall be deemed "works made for hire." To the extent that any such Work Product may not be considered a "work made for hire" under applicable law, Consultant hereby grants, transfers, assigns and conveys to COMPANY X and COMPANY X's clients an exclusive, paid-up, worldwide, perpetual license to 1) use, execute, reproduce, display, perform, distribute (internally and externally) copies of, and prepare derivative works based upon, such Work Product and derivative works thereof, and 2) authorize others to do any, some or all of the foregoing, such that COMPANY X and COMPANY X's clients may use and copy the Work Product and/or create derivative works from the Work Product unencumbered in any fashion by claims from the Consultant or a third party of the Consultant's and/or a third party's rights, title or interest in the Work Product or its underlying intellectual property.

(b) Consultant shall be free to use and employ its general skills, know-how and expertise, and to use, disclose and employ any generalized ideas, concepts, inventions, manuals, software, data files, know-how, methods, techniques or skills gained or learned during the course of the performance of any Services, so long as Consultant acquires and applies such information without the disclosure of any Proprietary Information and without any unauthorized use or disclosure of any Work Product. All ideas, concepts, inventions, manuals, software, data files, know-how, methods, techniques, skills and other intellectual property that Consultant has developed, created or acquired outside of performing the Services under this Agreement are and shall remain the sole and exclusive proprietary property of Consultant, except to the extent that rights are granted to COMPANY X and COMPANY X's clients as described in this clause.

WARRANTIES:
Consultant warrants that: (1) any and all representations made in resumes and other written or oral presentations to COMPANY X relating to Consultant's education, training, skills, work experience and similar matters are true and accurate; (2) all Services will be performed by Consultant utilizing the standards of care normally and customarily exercised by a professional performing comparable services under similar conditions; (3) Consultant has all requisite right and authority to enter into this Agreement with COMPANY X and that by doing so Consultant will not create any conflict of interest of any type, and should such conflict of interest later arise, shall provide COMPANY X with immediate notice of any such conflict of interest; (4) Consultant has no knowledge of any claims that would adversely affect Consultant's ability to assign all right, title and interest in and to the Work Product to COMPANY X; (5) the Work Product does not violate any patent, copyright or other proprietary right of any third party; and (6) Consultant has the legal right to grant COMPANY X the assignment of Consultant's interest in the Work Product as set forth in this Agreement.

INSURANCE:
Consultant shall obtain and maintain in full force and effect during the term of this Agreement

(1) commercial general liability insurance (including contractual liability coverage) with coverage limits of not less than Five Hundred Thousand ($500,000) per occurrence; (2) auto liability insurance with coverage limits of not less than One Million Dollars ($1,000,000) per occurrence; and (3) worker's compensation insurance as, and if, required by law. Consultant shall provide COMPANY X with a certificate of insurance evidencing the insurance coverages required under this clause when requested.

INDEMNIFICATION:
To the fullest extent permitted by law, Consultant shall indemnify, defend and hold COMPANY X and COMPANY X's clients harmless from and against any and all claims, demands, actions, suits proceedings, losses, damages, penalties, obligations, liabilities, costs and expenses (including, without limitation, reasonable attorneys' fees) arising directly or indirectly, in whole or in part from the negligence or willful misconduct of Consultant or the breach by Consultant of its obligations under this Agreement (including, without limitation, the breach of any warranty set forth under the clause entitled, "Warranty,") except to the extent arising from the sole negligence or willful misconduct of COMPANY X.

TERMINATION:
(a) Termination for Convenience
This Agreement may be terminated at any time in whole or in part for the convenience of COMPANY X by providing the Consultant with prior written notice. Such notice shall specify the extent to which the Agreement is being terminated, including which, and to what extent, current Task Orders are being terminated. Upon receipt of such notice, Consultant shall cease providing further Services as of the date of termination specified in the notice, advise COMPANY X of the extent to which Consultant has completed the Services through such termination date, and deliver to COMPANY X whatever Work Product then exists, and any physical embodiment thereof, in the manner requested by COMPANY X. COMPANY X shall make a final settlement payment to Consultant for all work performed through the date of such termination based on actual hours worked and actual expenses incurred if the work is being performed on a time and materials basis, or on a percent of completion if performed on a firm, fixed price basis.

(b) Termination for Default
(a) If either party fails to cure any breach of its obligations under this Agreement within ten (10) days following written notice from the other party, then such other party may terminate all or part of this Agreement, effective immediately, by providing the defaulting party with written notice of termination. Such written notice of termination shall specify the extent to which individual Task Orders are being terminated.

(b) If Consultant becomes bankrupt or otherwise insolvent, COMPANY X may, at its sole option and with written notice effective immediately, terminate this Agreement for default and pursue any other remedies available at law or in equity.

EXERCISE OF RIGHTS:
COMPANY X's failure to exercise any of its rights shall not constitute a waiver of any past, present or future right or remedy.

SURRENDER OF COMPANY X MATERIALS, DOCUMENTS, AND EQUIPMENT:
Upon the earlier of: (1) the termination of this Agreement, (2) the completion of a Task Order, or (3) a written demand by COMPANY X, Consultant shall promptly return to COMPANY X or to COMPANY X clients, as directed by COMPANY X, all documents, writings, tools, equipment and other materials made available to Consultant by COMPANY X and/or COMPANY X clients, or compiled or generated by Consultant in the course of performing Services hereunder, all of which shall be deemed to be the property of COMPANY X and/or of

its clients.

PROPRIETARY INFORMATION:
All proprietary, confidential and business information of COMPANY X and/or its clients including, but not limited to, information in tangible form marked with "Proprietary," "Confidential" or similar markings, specifications, processes, procedures, written documents, source code, capabilities, current or prospective products, services, customers or contracts, marketing strategies, research and development activities, and financial data ("Proprietary Information") shall be protected by the Consultant from disclosure to third parties. Any and all Proprietary Information shall be protected in the same manner and to the same degree that the Consultant protects its own proprietary information, but at a minimum will not: (1) disclose such Proprietary Information to any person unless authorized by COMPANY X in writing; (2) directly or indirectly use such Proprietary Information for Consultant's benefit or for that of any other business; and (3) will do all things reasonably required or requested by COMPANY X and/or COMPANY X's clients for the protection of such Proprietary Information. Consultant may use or disclose Proprietary Information that is or becomes publicly available, is already lawfully in Consultant's possession, is independently developed by Consultant, is lawfully obtained from third parties or the disclosing party has granted prior and specific written consent to the Consultant indicating the Proprietary Information may be disclosed to a third party. Protection of any such Proprietary Information shall continue for a period of seven (7) years following the termination of this Agreement in accordance with the "Termination" clause or the "Term" clause, as appropriate. The provisions of this clause shall survive the termination of this Agreement.

EXCUSED PERFORMANCE:
Neither party shall be liable for, and is excused from any failure to deliver or perform or for delay in delivery or performance due to causes beyond its reasonable control, including but not limited to, acts of nature, governmental actions, acts of war, fire, flood, labor difficulties, shortages, civil disturbances, transportation problems, interruptions of power or communications, or failure of suppliers.

NO HIRE:
In the event Consultant incorporates as a business entity and/or becomes capable of hiring staff, Consultant agrees not to hire, or to solicit for hire, any COMPANY X staff, including COMPANY X's other consultants, either as employees or contractors, during the term of this Agreement and for a period of one (1) year following the termination of this Agreement, without the prior written consent of COMPANY X. In addition, the Consultant agrees that during the term of this Agreement and for a period of one (1) year after the conclusion of a specific task order, Consultant will not accept the same work performed under a Task Order either directly or indirectly from COMPANY X's client, without the prior written consent of COMPANY X.

ASSIGNMENT OR TRANSFER:
Neither party to this Agreement may assign or transfer its interest in this Agreement to any other entity without prior written consent of the other party.

MODIFICATIONS:
Any modifications of this Agreement shall be in writing and executed by both COMPANY X and the Consultant.

AUDIT:
To the extent that actual costs or labor hours of personnel form the basis of payment under this Agreement, the Consultant shall provide to COMPANY X supporting documentation which is adequate to perform audit and verification of such actual costs and labor hours.

ORDER OF PRECEDENCE:

In the event of an inconsistency in this Agreement, unless otherwise provided herein, the inconsistency shall be resolved by giving precedence in the following order:

(a) Task Order's Price, Payment and Statement of Work Clauses
(b) This Agreement
(c) Other terms and conditions added to a Task Order
(d) Terms and conditions from a COMPANY X client contract incorporated by reference in a Task Order

APPLICABLE LAW:
This Agreement shall be governed by the laws of the Commonwealth of Virginia (Note: tailor to your particular region and laws).

IN WITNESS WHEREOF, THE PARTIES HAVE EXECUTED THIS AGREEMENT AS OF THE LAST DATE WRITTEN BELOW:

Consultant
Name of Business: Date:

Signature:

Printed Name:

Title:

EIN or SSN:

COMPANY X
Name of Business: COMPANY X, LLC   Date: December 3, 2015

Signature:
Printed Name:
John Doe

Title:

Company Logo   COMPANY X
Address
Email

EXHIBIT A: Statement of Work
The Consultant shall perform the Services described below when and if ordered under this Agreement via Task Orders:

1. Service Type
   Service Description

EXHIBIT B: Prices/Rates/Other Info

(a) The following labor rate shall be applicable to all work ordered under this Agreement: $0/hour

(b) Meals while in travel status shall be reimbursed at actual cost not to exceed a total of: $0/day

(c) Hotel expenses while in travel status shall be reimbursed at actual cost not to exceed: $0/day

(d) Mileage for Consultant's use of a personal car on behalf of COMPANY X business: $0/day

Company Logo   COMPANY X
Address
Email

EXHIBIT C: Sample Task Order

This Task Order is issued under the COMPANY X, LLC Consultant Agreement effective _____ between COMPANY X and:

Consultant Name:
Address:

Task Order No:
Task Order Type: T&M (or FFP)
Period of Performance: 00/00/0000 - 00/00/0000
Labor Rates: (If applicable, see Exhibit B)
Total Price or Total Estimated Cost: $
Payment Schedule (FFP only and if applicable):

Statement of Work:

Special Terms and Conditions Applicable Only to this Order:

(If the Special Terms and Conditions listed above include terms and conditions from a COMPANY X client, such terms and conditions shall be interpreted to read as follows: the name of the COMPANY X client shall mean "COMPANY X ," and the words "Contractor," "Supplier," "Vendor," "Consultant" or similar words shall mean the Consultant as defined in the main body of this Agreement. Any Special Terms and Conditions shall be applicable only to this Task Order and shall not apply to any other Task Order or to this Agreement as a whole unless specifically so stated.)

Consultant		COMPANY X	
Name of Business:	Date:	Name of Business:	Date:
Signature:		Signature:	
Printed Name:		Printed Name:	
Title:		Title:	

ABOUT THE AUTHOR

Chris Lutz is the founder and owner of S.P.A.R.T.A. With more than a decade of professional experience and a business owner, his business now provides other business owners with tools and resources to run more professional and organized operations.

Chris owns and consults for other businesses in all industries currently and is the author of several other books –

The Entrepreneur Lifestyle

Start, Operate, and Grow Your Personal Training Business

Metabolic Resistance Training

Maximum Fat Loss, Minimum Time

Is Your Healthy Diet Making You Fat? Why You Can't Seem to Lose Fat No Matter What You Do.

His website, www.theentrepreneurlifestyle.com is a celebration of the lifestyle of entrepreneurs and teaches them how to go from struggle to success with tools, eCourses, and other resources for entrepreneurs.

Chris' other website, www.lutzlures.com is an ecommerce site for the outdoor enthusiast and, specifically kayak fishermen.

www.ingramcontent.com/pod-product-compliance
Lightning Source LLC
Chambersburg PA
CBHW070809180526
45168CB00002B/546